30g

TIMELESS SPRING

TIMELESS

A WHEELWRIGHT PRESS Book

WEATHERHILL · *Tokyo* · *New York*

SPRING

A
Soto
Zen
Anthology

Edited and

Translated by Thomas Cleary

This book is published under the auspices of Wheelwright Press, the publishing arm of Zen Center, 300 Page Street, San Francisco, California 94102. The Press selects and edits material to be published and then, as in the present case, asks a trade publisher to undertake the actual distribution of the book.

Published by John Weatherhill, Inc., of New York and Tokyo, with editorial offices at 7-6-13 Roppongi, Minato-ku, Tokyo 106, Japan. Copyright in Japan 1980 by Wheelwright Press, all rights reserved. Printed in Japan.

Library of Congress Catalog Card No. 78-146753
Library of Congress Cataloging in Publication Data
Timeless Spring.
"A Wheelwright Press Book."
    1. Soto (Sect)—Addresses, essays, lectures.
    2. Priests, Zen—Japan—Biography.
I. Cleary, Thomas F., 1949–.
BQ9416.T55   294.3'927   79-26677
ISBN 0-8348-0148-5

CONTENTS

5

Foreword

I want to express my gratitude to Dr. Thomas Cleary for his compassionate understanding of and great care in translating these records of a zen buddhist lineage.

And I want to express my gratitude to my teacher Shunryu Suzuki-roshi, an heir of this lineage.

How are we to understand these stories and biographies as teachings? To really recognize these stories, this lineage as your own face, you yourself will have to practice. Practice is to recognize and act on the truth of each moment. Or rather practice is to try to practice, to try to act on the truth of each moment. This book can be a teacher as can be everything around you if you know how to bring things to life, to truth — if you know how to tap everyday life.

One day when Guishan Lingyou was attending Baizhang, Baizhang asked, "Who are You?"

"I am Lingyou."

Baizhang, "Will you look in the brazier and see if there are any hot coals left."

Guishan looked and poked around, "No, there are none."

Baizhang got up, took the tongs and poked deep into the fire pot. He came up with a glowing charcoal. "Is this not a hot coal?"

With this Guishan awakened. He had known he was only provisionally Lingyou, but he was not the one who found the hot coal. He had not understood that emptiness is form.

Baizhang said, "The method I just used is only for this occasion. It is not the usual approach. To realize our buddha-nature, we must wait for the right moment and the right conditions. When the time comes it is like awakening from a dream, as if something long forgotten was remembered. We realize that what is obtained is our own and not from outside ourselves."

How can we extract the hot coals from this book?

Dogen-zenji said, "Please keep in mind that the buddhas and patriarchs express their real selves in the everyday activities of drinking tea and eating rice." He also said, "Do not think that there is no drinking of tea or eating of rice after taking a meal. This is meaningful study. There is no buddhist way besides this. We must not seek to borrow the power of the buddhas and patriarchs."

Zhaozhou asked, "What is the way?"
Nanquan said, "Everydaymindedness is the way."
"Is it possible to approach it?"
"If you approach it intentionally, you will miss it."

A poem:

Although what our eyes see is ordinary
And does not frighten people,
It remains like moonlight on a chilled window.
Even in the middle of the night
It shines upon thatched cottages.

This book should not be read just as a collection of essays by different people. The third patriarch, Sengcan, was a layman; the fourth patriarch, Daoxin, a priest. From the point of view of transmission they are one person, both realized as one person — a difference only of strategies, expression, leaf and air, simultaneous points of view.

In Chinese paintings over the centuries, the layman's costume changes from age to age, while the monk's remains the same. The layman feels like his contemporaries; and the monk, as well as being contemporary, feels like those who came before and those who will come after. The nature of our life is to be replaced, waves, child succeeding parent, generation succeeding generation. Merit (the buddhist concept of accumulated virtue or endowment) is to lead a life you would offer to your children, to your friends, to your descendants,

9

even to your ancestors. And yet lineage, sangha, links you to your contemporaries by the commitment to mutual understanding.

Dogen-zenji says, "Lineage is not like many different things put in a line or gathered together." Lineage is a succession of one moment without time or space, the simultaneity and power of the sky of spring, a timeless spring, that in the same time unites history through the personal sincerity of each successor. Eighty-eight people join Suzuki-roshi and the historical Shakyamuni Buddha who lived more than two thousand five hundred years ago. These ninety persons probably understand, know each other better than any ninety contemporary persons know each other.

A teacher is a person who waits for you outside your agenda, outside the script into which you are always trying to write the world. The disciple is a homeleaver, water without a course. But water has the power, which cannot be taken away from it, to find its own course. Each disciple, each committed student of buddhism, is water finding its own course. This course is entered and renewed by a life of sustained awareness, personal integrity, and nonattachment. It is a stream that carries from Buddha until the present day.

The buddhist haiku poet, Basho, said that the poet must be empty and direct enough to become one with the source of inspiration on every moment — and expression should feel effortless and have a sense of eternity. This is to express the particular without violating the absolute, to tap everyday life. It is in this sincerity of each moment we find our own unique flowering. The rare and true gift. Each moment is unrepeatable, unpredictable, and uniquely simultaneous with other events. The entire universe is just one direction, neither east nor west, nor up nor down.

This is the path that is the space between our fingers, before our noses, the path for which there are no guides other than our spontaneous unhesitating intention — our actual life of nonattachment by which we see the real form of the world, by which we find the fullness of the experience we have now without fear or possessiveness. This is called treading the hidden path, or meeting no one on the ancient road. You will find that conscience is the root, purity, and clarity of consciousness. And when the given is not taken for granted, you will find practice and the use of necessity.

Please try to read these stories as if the words were intended directly for you. These stories are meant to become your own stories, your own life. Do not read them with the speed and distance of your conceptual mind. Read them with your body and breath, as if you were to read aloud or chant or write or calligraph each word. Read as if you were accepted by each of these teachers. You are accepted. Open yourself to the power of respect and others' expectations. Accept others and let others accept you. Then you will be in the midst of lineage, in the midst of the power of everyone.

What does everyone expect of you — if possible, they want you to be a buddha. And it is possible. These teachers do and would accept you, more than you accept yourself. Many histories unlock in your every act. Reading this book you may be looking at your own lineage, your own grandparents. To become accessible to the lineage is to become the treasure from which nothing is excluded. One of your histories is that of Buddha. The pin-up that never lets you down, the person that everyone would like you to be, your fullest and widest personality, we call Buddha. Buddha is the name, the instruction that is the act of living. The thought of each being is the thought of enlightenment.

These stories are not a matter of knowing or not knowing, or even understanding. You cannot see the bottom of the ocean even if you could dry up the ocean. Wuzu Fayan asked, "If you meet a man of zen on the way, and greet him with neither words nor with silence, tell me, how will you greet him?" Fayan began studying buddhism when he was thirty-five years old. One day he read, 'It is said in buddhism that when a bodhisattva sees with his satori eye, working and principle are fused, circumstances and essence are unified, subjectivity and objectivity are not separated. A non-

11

buddhist scholar argued with this, because if subjectivity and objectivity are not separated, nothing can be proved. But the teacher answered that it is the same as if one realizes personally how cold or warm water is by drinking it oneself.' Fayan thought to himself, "I know cold and warm, but what is it to realize 'personally?' "

Dr. Cleary has compiled and translated this book so that you can meet these great masters and yourself personally. They are not buddhists, they are buddhism. And when you meet your own life personally, in person, each moment, you are buddhism. The fleeting smile of a baby. On what will you act? On what moments has your life turned? What has been the joy, the movement of your life?

Great teacher Shitou Xiqian once said, "I live in a hermitage that contains nothing of value. After taking my meal, if I feel sleepy, I nap."

Great teacher Dogen-zenji said, "We have to accept that in this world there are millions and millions of objects and each one respectively is the entire world. This is where the study of buddhism begins."

This is an English text and lineage of the Zen Buddhist school. Dr. Cleary has exposed the embers, please fan them yourselves.

Zentatsu Baker
Abbot, San Francisco Zen Center
1979

Translator's Introduction

Chan, or zen buddhism, has been called the school of the enlightened mind, the true school of no attachment, the gate of the source, the fundamental vehicle; it teaches direct insight into the essence of mind, realization of its ineffable nature, and awakening of its dormant capacities. In its deepest sense, chan is not a school of buddhism but the inner meaning of buddhism, the science of enlightenment; outwardly it presents psycho-physical technology for unlocking the secret of fundamental enlightenment. In speaking of chan and zen, therefore, it must be borne in mind that both transcendent and relative aspects are referred to, whether it be primarily one or the other or both equally.

The origins of chan in China were from among people like the Mahasiddhas in the Indian sphere and the Sufis from Central Asia to Europe, who were dedicated to actualizing the living meaning of the teachings of the sacred scriptures and traditions of the sages. More or less alienated from priestly or monastic bureaucracy, token ritualism and literalist scholarship, originally they were often scorned, even persecuted, for nonconformity and nondogmatic, even antidogmatic speech and action; eventually they became the most vibrant spiritual forces in their world areas.

By the end of the seventh century, chan masters were being celebrated as 'Teachers of the Nation of China,' and chan was being taught and practiced all over China, in large urban centers as well as remote rural areas. This was two centuries after Bodhidharma, an Indian monk considered to be the first patriarch of chan in China; it was still

13

several centuries before the peak of the profuse flowering of chan literature which grew up through the heritage of the eminent Tang and Sung dynasty masters.

During the Tang dynasty, which lasted from the seventh through the ninth centuries, a number of monks and scholars came from Japan to study in China, as the political and cultural influence of the Tang empire was being felt all the way from the kingdoms of Annam, Nanchao, and Tibet in the south and west, among the Turkic and Mongolian federations in the west and north, through the nations of Korea and Japan in the north and east. Although this was the time of the later chan patriarchs and the subsequent rise of the so-called Five Houses, sometimes considered to be the golden age of chan, the Japanese pilgrims did not seem to make much, if any, contact with the mainstreams of chan activity at this time. The pilgrims studied mostly in the capital areas or ancient monastic centers on famous mountains, where the doctrinal schools of buddhism were active; chan was largely scattered throughout mountainous areas of southern China, far from the traditional homeland of Chinese civilization. Early in the ninth century one pilgrim did, however, make contact with two streams of chan which became extinct not long after in China; he transmitted their teachings to Japan, including it among the four transmissions of Japanese Tendai buddhism. This teaching was revived for a time in Japan in the twelfth and thirteenth centuries as the Bodhidharma sect or buddha mind sect; many of the members of this school eventually became disciples of zen master Dogen, who in 1227 returned from China as an enlightened successor of the chan transmission.

During the Sung dynasty, from the tenth to the thirteenth century, chan and Pure Land buddhism were in effect the only buddhist movements surviving the government persecutions of the ninth and tenth centuries; most of the leading buddhist teachers of the times were chan masters, who often were well versed in the scriptural schools of buddhism and even learned in confucianism. A number of chan masters also cultivated and encouraged Pure Land practice of Buddha name invocation; this trend grew in popularity later on. Many chan masters were excellent poets, calligraphers, scholars and speakers, and many secular poets, artists, and scholars practiced chan meditation and sought the association and instruction of chan adepts. Hence during the Sung dynasty, continuing the trend of the Tang, chan made a tremendous impact on Chinese culture. Even now, the ancient chan dictum of "no work, no food" and the practice of sitting meditation for therapeutic calming of mind and body are still in evidence in China, where the last vestiges of buddhism as a religion have been virtually obliterated.

Under the Sung dynasty a system of public chan monasteries, known as the Five Mountains and Ten Fields, was organized and run under officially recognized monastic regulations. In former ages, the chan schools were continually scattering, as enlightened successors left the parent school to continue traveling or to live in anonymity until circumstances exposed them to the opportunity to teach; whether a monastery was maintained or not as a focus of chan practice depended on the presence of a teaching master. Under the Five Mountain and Ten Field system, a vacant abbacy in one of these large public monasteries was filled by consulting the well known chan masters in the land to find a suitable replacement from among the chan adepts. This system avoided the projection of sectarianism on the variety of chan lineages, but unavoidabily exposed people to the trap of institutionalization and competition that pristine chan had broken away from earlier, after buddhism became in effect the state religion of China. In both China and Japan, however, while eminent masters appeared from time to time in the famous monasteries, attracting huge numbers of students, the transmission was continuing outside of the religious, cultural, and political centers as well.

15

As in China, where chan came to light after centuries of buddhist influence, so too in Japan zen took root and grew on its own after long experience with the scriptural schools of buddhism. Most students of chan in China and zen in Japan were familiar with the major buddhist scriptures, and as time went on, many steeped themselves in the literature of chan-zen tradition. Several of the pre-Tang patriarchs of Tientai buddhism and Tang patriarchs of Huayen buddhism were recognized as chan masters, and two eminent Sung dynasty chan masters are recognized as patriarchs of Pure Land buddhism, as these various traditions were always in contact. In Japan, most of the early zen students and the Japanese masters were deeply learned in the exoteric and esoteric Tendai buddhist teachings; in later times many practitioners of Buddha name recitation came to hear the teachings of the zen masters, and a number of zen masters also taught and practiced the invocation of Amitabha Buddha. The source of chan and the Teachings is one; the vaunted iconoclasm of chan and zen is a practical application of the adage that "when the illness is gone, the medicine is removed," which applies to chan teaching as well — as the saying of a famous master goes, "we have no sayings — there is no doctrine to give people."

The chan patriarchy seems to have been obscure until the time of the fourth patriarch Daoxin (580-651). The founding father, Bodhidharma, is thought by some to have been one of the Mahasiddhas; a yoga master, he came to China at a very advanced age, after having taught in India for fifty years, and spent another fifty years in various parts of China, teaching as the occasion arose. Near the end of his life he went to Shaolin monastery in northwest China and sat for nine years facing a wall; this is one of the primary ways in which he is remembered in illustrative zen history. The second patriarch (Huike 487-593) had studied confuciansim and taoism, finally turning to buddhism; after eight years in meditation he went to see

Bodhidharma and stayed there at Shaolin for another six years, becoming the foremost of Bodhidharma's few known disciples. The second patriarch communicated the chan transmission of the seal of the enlightened mind to ten disciples, several of whom were laymen, including Sengcan (d. 606), who was to be the third patriarch. Tradition says that Sengcan did not communicate it to anyone except Daoxin, but he is also said to be the author of the *Shin-shin-ming*, a poem on faith in the mind, which may rightfully be called the first chan classic, widely appreciated for more than a thousand years.

The fourth patriarch Daoxin established the first self-sufficient chan mountain center, as more than five hundred students gathered around him; he wrote books on meditation and bodhisattva precepts and became the first nationally known chan father. Daoxin also is noted for setting the example of not obeying the imperial summons to the capital. Daoxin's only successor, Hongren (602-675), continued to teach on the same mountain, on a different peak, and eventually produced eleven enlightened disciples, a number of whom became prominent teachers. Huineng (638-713), perhaps the most famous of the patriarchs, had over forty successors, and was the source of the streams of chan that were to continue the mind to mind communication of chan for over a millennium.

According to the classic chan history *Transmission of the Lamp,* the foremost of Huineng's disciples was chan master Xingsi of Qingyuan mountain (d.740). In a dialogue that later became a well known chan public case, he asked the patriarch, "What should be done so as not to fall into stages?" The patriarch said, "What have you done?" He said, "I don't even strive at the holy truths." The patriarch said, "Then what stage do you fall into?" He said, "If even the holy truths are not practiced, what stages are there?" The patriarch said, "So it is, so it is. Keep it well."

Despite the great popularity of the sixth patriarch, as many of his heirs lived in obscurity, the flourishing of chan is said to have started with Shitou (700-790) and Mazu (709-788). Mazu was the successor of Nanyue (677-744), another of Huineng's enlightened disciples, while Shitou was the successor of the aforementioned Qingyuan (as Xingsi is known, according to custom, after a place he lived). Mazu and Shitou came to be called the "two gates of elixir," and their enlightened disciples spread throughout China.

In his boyhood, Shitou showed an unusual character, once destroying a sacrificial altar in an aboriginal village and leading away an ox that was to be killed. Later he went to meet the sixth patriarch and was ordained as a disciple; before he had received full ordination, the patriarch died and the boy was directed to Qingyuan, eventually to become his foremost disciple and sole heir. Subsequently he went to Hengyue (also called Nanyue), one of the holy mountains of China, and built a hut on a flat boulder beside a temple there; because of this he came to be known as Shitou Heshang, "The Monk on the Rock." Shitou's famous composition *Merging of Difference and Unity* is a seminal work of chan dialectic, highly appreciated and subject to numerous ancient and modern commentaries.

Shitou had twenty one enlightened successors, from whom three of the five houses of chan were descended — the Cao-Dong, Yunmen, and Fayen. Shitou's heir Tienhuang Daowu, from whom the latter two chan houses were descended, also succeeded to Mazu, as did a number of eminent chan masters of the time.

Most of the masters in the third generation of Shitou's lineage were disciples of Yaoshan Weiyen (745-828). Once Shitou said, "Speech and movement are irrelevant," and Yaoshan responded, "Not speaking or moving is also irrelevant." Shitou said, "Here a needle cannot be pushed in." Yaoshan said, "Here is like planting flowers on a rock." Shitou deeply approved of him. There is a famous verse, often quoted in chan literature, which was originally composed by Shitou in praise of Yaoshan:

Though we've been dwelling together, I don't know
    his name:
Going along accepting the flow, just being thus,
Even the eminent sages since antiquity don't know
    him –
How could the hasty ordinary type presume to
understand?

Once as Yaoshan was reading a scripture, master Baiyan, one of Mazu's successors, said to him, "You should stop fooling people." Yaoshan rolled up the text and said, "What time of day is it?" Baiyan said, "Just noon." Yaoshan said, "There's still this pattern." Baiyan said, "I don't even have nothing." Yaoshan said, "You are too brilliant." Baiyan said, "I am just thus; what about you?" Yaoshan said, "I limp along, ungainly in a hundred ways, clumsy in a thousand, still I go on this way."

Yunyan Tansheng (781-841) studied with Baizhang Huaihai (720-814) for twenty years, serving as his attendant. Baizhang was a leading successor of Mazu and is credited with the formal establishment of the unique chan monastic system. After Baizhang's death, Yunyan went to Yaoshan, where he soon became enlightened. Among Yunyan's own chan successors was the reknowned Dongshan Liangjie (807-869), who came to be honored as the father of one of the Five Houses of classical chan buddhism.

Dongshan began to study buddhism as a boy; taught to recite the popular Heart of Wisdom scripture, which says there are no eye, ear, nose, etc. he felt his face and asked his teacher why the scripture said there are none, when he had them. The scripture means that the senses, their fields and consciousnesses, have no independent natures and cannot be grasped, and the teacher, realizing he could not solve this problem for the boy, sent him to a chan master, Lingmo (746-818), one of Mazu's disciples. At the age of twenty one Dongshan was fully ordained and went traveling for enlightenment. He first called on Nanquan (747-834), one of Mazu's latest and greatest successors; while still a young monk, Dongshan became highly respected in the community of his eminent master.

Subsequently Dongshan called on Guishan Lingyou (771-853) and asked about the saying of a past master that inanimate objects expound the Dharma. Dharma means the teaching, here the buddhist, or enlightening teaching, and it also means principle, quality, and phenomena; it is said that all dharmas, all things, are enlightening dharmas. Guishan lifted his whisk and asked Dongshan if he heard it; Dongshan didn't understand, and asked what scripture the expression came from. Guishan cited the saying of the *Hua Yen,* or Flower Garland scripture, that all things in all worlds in all times expound the Dharma. Finally Dongshan asked Guishan to direct him to another man of the way, and Guishan, who had been a disciple of Baizhang, told him about Yunyan.

When Dongshan questioned Yunyan, Yunyan told him that the insentient could hear the inanimate preaching. The ancient master had explained to his original questioner, "Right now in the midst of all activities, if there is just no arising and disappearance of the twin streams of ordinary and holy, this is subtle consciousness which clearly perceives without belonging to either existence or nonexistence; you just perceive without hangups and attachments to feelings and consciousness. That is why the sixth patriarch said, 'The six senses discriminating in reference to objects is not consciousness.'" Dongshan asked Yunyan if he could hear the inanimate teaching; Yunyan said, "If I heard it, you wouldn't hear my teaching." Yunyan said, "If you don't even hear my teaching, how can you hear the teaching of the inanimate?" According to one version, Dongshan then presented his understanding to Yunyan in a verse, but another version has it that he again asked Yunyan what scripture the teaching of the inanimate was based on, and Yunyan cited the Amitabha scripture saying that all the rivers, birds, trees and forests invoke Buddha and Dharma, whereupon Dongshan understood and presented the verse, saying,

> *Wonderful! Wonderful!*
> *The sermon of the inanimate is inconceivable.*
> *If you try to hear it with your ears*
> *After all you'll hardly understand*
> *Only when you hear it in your eyes*
> *Will you be able to know.*

Baizhang has spoken of the inanimate, or insentient, having buddha-nature in similar terms, explaining "insentience" as a metaphor for non-attachment; he says, "Right now, in regard to the two spheres of ordinary and holy, and all things, existent or nonexistent, just have no grasping or rejecting mind at all, and also have no knowledge or understanding of not grasping or rejecting; this is called insentient having buddha-nature. It is just that there is no bondage by feelings, that is why it is called insentience."

After Dongshan left Yunyan, he still had some doubt, until one day he happened to see his reflection when he looked into a river as he crossed over and was suddenly greatly enlightened. Then he uttered his famous verse,

> *Just don't seek from another*
> *Or you'll be far estranged from self.*
> *I now go on alone*
> *Meeting it everywhere*
> *It now is just what I am*
> *I now am not it.*
> *You must comprehend in this way*
> *To merge with thusness.*

Not seeking anything outside of fundamental completeness, one realizes the self that is self because there is no other, and the self that is no self because there is no other. In harmony with nature, seeing reality — thusness —

21

everywhere, yet one does not identify, remaining fluid and free, not pinned down to anything. Zen master Keizan explained, "If you know you go by yourself alone wherever you are, you accord with all suchness as is. Therefore an ancient said, 'There is no knowledge outside of suchness that is proved by suchness, no suchness outside of knowledge that is cultivated by knowledge.' Suchness is immutable, it is clear constant eternal knowledge; therefore it is said that completely illumined knowledge does not depend on thought."

Dongshan continued to travel for many years, famed throughout the monasteries as a school in himself; toward the end of his life he stayed and taught at Xinfeng Mountain and later at Dong Mountain (Dongshan), by which name he is known to posterity. Dongshan had twenty six successors, and his lineage came to be called the Dong succession, or the Cao-Dong school, after Dongshan and his great disciple Caoshan. Dongshan's long poem *Song of the Jewel Mirror Awareness*, is, like Shitou's *Merging of Difference and Unity*, a seminal classic, and contains the matrix of the "five ranks" teaching design associated with the Cao-Dong tradition.

Among Dongshan's numerous successors were two outstanding teachers of the age; Caoshan Benji (840-901) and Yunju Daoying (d.902). Caoshan originally studied confucianism, then left home at age nineteen to become a monk. He met Dongshan late in the latter's life, and visited him repeatedly to ask for guidance. He stayed around Dongshan for several years and was especially skilful at expounding chan in terms of Dongshan's 'five ranks' device, making commentaries on Dongshan's verses on the five ranks as well as other formulations of chan processes. Caoshan's final conversation with Dongshan succinctly captures the teaching of integration of absolute and relative that is at the heart of the five ranks: when Caoshan took leave of him, Dongshan asked, "Where are you going?" Caoshan said, "To an unchanging place." Dongshan said, "If it's an unchanging place, how could there be any going?" Caoshan said, "Going too is unchanging."

Yunju's community of disciples is said to have always numbered fifteen hundred people; he wrote nothing, and relatively few of his sayings are left to posterity, but the succession of Dongshan lived on through Yunju's lineage after those of Dongshan's other heirs had died out. Yunju's sayings are forceful and direct, and he does not touch upon the five ranks as a formulated system.

By the fifth generation of Dongshan's lineage there were only a few known chan masters of the Cao-Dong style left, and most of them left no successors. Dayang Qingxuan, an outstanding teacher descended from Yunju, had fifteen enlightened disciples, but all of them died before he did. An outstanding chan master, Fushan Fayuan, an intrepid pilgrim and successor to two great Linji chan masters, came to see Dayang; as they were in accord, Dayang entrusted Fushan with finding a successor for him and preserving the Cao-Dong style of chan transmission. Later Dayang passed the bequest of Dayang on to an enlightened student, Touzi Yiqing, from whom all subsequent generations of chan masters bearing the Cao-Dong transmission are descended.

In the *Five Lamps Merged in the Source,* a standard chan collection of the thirteenth century, we find much more material on Dayang, Touzi, and his successors, than of the masters since Dongshan and Caoshan. Touzi made a collection of one hundred public cases of chan records, summing up each with a simple verse of his own. In the latter thirteenth century chan master Linquan Conglun gave a series of talks on his collection, adding introductions, remarks and lectures, in the fashion of the well-known classic *Blue Cliff Record.* This was recorded, to become the *Empty Valley Collection.* Later Linquan gave similar talks on a collection of one hundred cases with verses by Danxia Zichun (d. 1119), successor to one of Touzi's heirs, producing the *Vacant Hall Collection.*

23

Touzi's most distinguished successor was the great Furong Daokai (1042-1118). He asked Touzi, "The sayings of the buddhas and patriarchs are like everyday food and drink: apart from this, is there any special way to help people?" Touzi said, "You tell me, does the command of the emperor in his realm depend on the ancient kings?" As Furong was about to speak, Touzi hit him in the mouth with his whisk and said, "As soon as you produce an idea, already you've got thirty blows of the cane." At this Furong awakened.

Furong became an outstanding chan teacher of the age, and was abbot at the large public monastery of Tienning until he was exiled for declining imperial honors. Furong, the mountain after which he is usually known, was his abode in exile; there he delivered an address to the assembly which was canonized as the *Standards of Jetavana,* with fundamental guidelines for the spiritual community, harkening back to the time of Shakyamuni Buddha in the Jeta Grove. Furong's teaching flourished, and he had twenty six enlightened disciples.

Danxia Zichun, successor to Furong, the poet of the *Vacant Hall Collection,* was teacher of Changlu Zhenxie Qingliao (n.d.) and Tiantong Hongzhi Zhenjue (1091-1153), two outstanding chan masters. The record of Hongzhi is far larger than any other Cao-Dong chan master in China. When he was abbot at the great monastery at Tiantong mountain, students came from all over, swelling the ranks of the community to over fifteen hundred. Included in Hongzhi's record are hundreds of comments and poems on ancient chan stories and sayings. A later master, Wansong Xingxiu (1166-1246) lectured on two collections of one hundred cases each, made by Hongzhi. One, with Hongzhi's poems, became the nucleus of the *Book of Equanimity,* and the other, with Hongzhi's prose comments, became the nucleus of the *Record of Further Inquiries;* the former is designed like the *Blue Cliff Record* while the latter consists of the ancient story, Hongzhi's remarks with Wansong's comments and talks.

Wansong studied chan first with master Shengmo, who told him, "Studying this path is like refining gold; when it's impure, the pure gold doesn't show. As I look between your eyebrows, there is very much something there. If you don't 'pierce through cold bones' once, you won't be able to cast this thing off. Hereafter, see for yourself; it is not a matter of my speaking much." And Shengmo had him contemplate Changsha's saying, to turn yourself back into the mountains, rivers, and earth. For six months he couldn't get into it. Shengmo said, "I only hope you'll understand late." After a long time, one day he suddenly had insight, but he still couldn't understand why an ancient master had said of the monk who was enlightened upon seeing peach blossoms, "Quite right, but I dare say the old brother isn't through yet."

Eventually Wansong went to Xueyuan, a sixth generation successor in Furong's line, where he became greatly enlightened. He said, "It is so near — all my former cleverness burnt up in one fire, for the first time I see how Shengmo helped people." In his talks on chan cases, Wansong quotes Shengmo as well as Xueyuan, telling what they said about the stories. Wansong stayed with Xueyuan for two more years investigating the subtleties, and finally was entrusted with carrying on the teaching. From that time on he became famous; in 1193, at the age of twenty seven, he was summoned by the emperor of the Jin dynasty, the Jurchen rulers of northern China. Later he served as abbot of several monasteries by imperial appointment under the Jurchen Jin and Mongol Yuan dynasties. In his latter years he retired to the House of Equanimity, after which his best known work is named.

Rujing (1163-1228), a contemporary of Wansong, was another famous chan master who served as teaching abbot of several of the public monasteries, but it was not known who his chan teacher was until at the end of his life he revealed that he had acknowledgement of the transmission from Xuedou Zhijian, a descendant of Danxia Zichun. Rujing's practice was just sitting; he lived in a monastery from the age of nineteen, gave up the study of scriptures, never returned to his native place, never spoke to the villagers, not even to people next to him in the monk's hall, didn't go to any of the various halls and rooms but just sat in the monks' meditation hall, vowing to wear out a diamond seat. He said, "No more need to burn incense, make prostrations, invoke buddhas, perform repentence ceremonies, or read scriptures — just sit and liberate mind and body."

There were several enlightened people in Rujing's assembly, including the famous Japanese zen master Dogen (1200-1253), who inherited the patched robe of Furong. Dogen was a profound scholar of the buddhist teachings and also practiced Rinzai (Linji) zen in Japan for nine years before he and his zen teacher went to China in 1223 to seek further guidance. After traveling around to various monasteries, hearing the teachings and meeting the chan abbots, Dogen saw Rujing at last and stayed to study with him. There Dogen sat still day and night, and finally became greatly enlightened. After two more years with Rujing, in 1227 Dogen returned to Japan, where he taught and wrote and is considered the first patriarch of Soto (Cao-Dong) zen.

Dogen spent about ten years living in various places, then spent another ten years at Kosho Horin temple near Kyoto, where a group of students began to gather around him. It was during these years that Dogen gave the talks collected by his disciple Ejo under the title *Record of Things Heard from the Treasury of the Eye of the True Teaching*. In his last years he lived at Eiheiji, the monastery he founded in the mountainous snow country, facing the China Sea.

Dogen endeavored to recrystallize the ancient verities of buddhism. He criticized the decadent tendencies of past and present, wrote principles and rules for monastic organization and conduct, made detailed analyses of many significant passages from scriptures and chan lore, commented on hundreds of public cases, wrote and delivered numerous talks on the fundamentals of zen practice. He especially emphasized the unity of practice and realization, that true practice is not seeking, but practice of realization, and particularly exhorted pure sitting. Like the founding fathers of chan in China, Dogen was opposed by members of established groups, and his teaching was not so widespread in his time as was his influence through his descendants, but he left a tremendous body of writings and speeches which have inspired zen students for seven centuries.

In Soto zen tradition Dogen is known as The Eminent Ancestor, and the fourth generation patriarch, Keizan Jokin (1268-1325) is known as The Great Ancestor, as it was with him that Soto zen began to flourish, with his zen successors spreading the way throughout Japan. Keizan taught as abbot at several monasteries, then finally walked off to roam till the end of his life, teaching according to the occasion as crowds of people came to see him. Keizan also wrote many works; his treatise on sitting meditation and his *Esoteric Shobogenzo,* a set of ten zen stories with Keizan's reflections, are intended to convey his teaching in quintessential form.

According to Geppa Doin (1644- ?), one of the eminent Soto teachers of the Tokugawa period revival of zen in Japan, the school of Dogen, from its beginnings in the 1230's and 40's, flourished from the late 1200's to the early 1400's, faded in the mid-fifteenth century, declined after the late fifteenth century, and had been continuing weakly for two hundred years. Geppa's *Biographical Extracts of the Original Stream* chronicles the highlights of the succession of his lineage through twenty-four generations from Dogen to the seventeenth century zen master Guon, Geppa's final teacher. As zen is not a doctrinal school but a succession of living exemplars, the chain of transmission has a profound meaning in zen which has nothing to do with school or sect. This book is both conventional and illustrative history, tracing evidence of the communication of the inmost mind of zen through the vicissitudes of centuries.

Zen method is often described in terms of dying and returning to life; as Shitou said, a sage has no self, but there is nothing that is not himself. This is analagous to the development from the individual lesser vehicle to the collective greater vehicle of buddhism; according to the *Mahaparinirvana* scripture,

It is like when a woman rears an infant and the infant gets sick, she worries and looks for a doctor. When the doctor arrives he compounds three kinds of medicine . . . and gives it to the child to take; then he tells the women not to breast-feed the child until the medicine has been digested.

Then the woman paints her breasts with bitter taste and tells the infant, 'My breasts are covered with poison; don't touch them anymore.' The infant thirsts for her milk, but hearing that the milk is poisonous, it gives up and goes away.

When the medicine has been digested, the mother then washes her breasts and calls the child to give it milk. Now the infant, though it hungers and thirsts again, having heard before it is poisonous, therefore doesn't come.

The mother now says, 'Because you had taken medicine, I painted my breasts with poison; now that your medicine is dispersed, I have washed — so now you can drink milk with no trouble.' After hearing this, the infant gradually comes back to drink.

Good people, the buddhas are also like this: for the transcendence of all, they teach sentient beings to cultivate the state of selflessness. Having thus cultivated, they forever end the selfish mind and enter *nirvana*. This is to get rid of all conventional false views, and to show a truth which goes beyond the world, and also to show that the conventional idea of self is false and not truly real; to cultivate pure body of the selfless state. Just as the woman, for the sake of her child, painted her breasts with bitter flavor, so too do the buddhas, for the sake of the cultivation of emptiness, say that all things have no self. Just as the woman, having washed her breasts, calls her child to bring it back to drink, so too does the buddha speak of the womb of the realization of thusness.

Therefore mendicants should not be afraid — like that little child, hearing its mother's call, coming back gradually to drink, so should the mendicants discern for themselves the hidden treasury of the realization of thusness, which must be there.

In the ancient scriptures we read that the Buddha taught all sorts of meditations, from absorption in colors to such refined states as formless absorptions in infinite space, infinite consciousness, nothingness, beyond cognition and noncognition, and even the end of sensation and perception. Yet none of these is *nirvana*, none is a goal in the buddhist context; they are means of freeing mind and body from routine and habitual thought and activity, to open the practitioner to the possibility of *nirvana*, the turning point of the enlightened life.

By shedding attachments to things and thoughts, one may come to realize that they have no binding nature, that value systems are originally mental constructions; the miraculous ability to "change earth to gold and gold to earth" spoken of in zen texts represents such freedom in the world. If the naive realistic view is not shattered by transcendent wisdom and the sublime meditative states themselves are made objects of attachment, forever pitted against the affairs of the mundane world, true enlightenment and liberation cannot take place. When the mentally constructed facade of identity projected on persons and things is dropped, there is only "thusness" — as Yaoshan said, "Now that I've shed my skin completely, only one true reality alone is there."

When the fourth patriarch first came to the third patriarch, it is said, he was asked what he was seeking; when he replied that he sought liberation, the third patriarch simply said, "Who binds you?" The fourth patriarch replied that no one was binding him, whereupon the third patriarch said, "Then why seek liberation?" At

29

this the fourth patriarch's mind opened. Similarly, the later chan master Guishan would say, "If feelings do not attach to things, how can things hinder people?"

But not being attached is easier said than done, and therefore considerable emphasis is often placed on what is called in the teachings the "gate of sweeping away" and in zen the "killing sword." There are many passages in buddhist texts which exhaust the possibilities of human life and show the pithless nature of our doings, to help us agree to loosen intellectual and emotional bonds. In the famous parable of the *Lotus* scripture, the children are too involved in playing with their toys to notice that the house is on fire; so their father promises them better toys, *nirvana* and liberation, if they will come out of the house.

In the scriptures of great vehicle buddhism, extinct *nirvana* is called "the illusory citadel," used to relieve fatigue and despair on confronting the endless way; it is also called "the deep pit of liberation" and "reducing the body to ashes, obliterating knowledge," as its ineffable serenity is so intoxicating that one may utterly forget the mundane world and never return. There are many analagous terms and sayings in zen literature, warning against one-sided views, putting the "great death" in perspective as part of a process. In the *Lotus* scripture it says that it is those in whom desire rages who seek peace and quiet as bliss; in the great way, the middle way, there is neither grasping nor rejection.

Transcending the world in its very midst, being in the world but not of it, one might call a hallmark of the buddhist way. If zen teaching seems paradoxical, perhaps it is just because it presents both poles, "the solitary peak" and "the bustling market place," and deals with subtle levels of integration. In principle, Caoshan explains it this way:

The absolute state is the realm of emptiness, where fundamentally there is not a single thing. The relative state is the realm of form, where there are myriad images and shapes. The relative in the absolute turns from noumenon to phenomena; the absolute in the relative relinquishes phenomena and enters noumenon: mutual integration mysteriously responds to myriad circumstances without falling into the various states of existence; it is not defiled or pure, not absolute or relative: therefore it is called the empty mysterious great way, the true school of no attachment.

As a practical process by which one achieves this, Caoshan says that at first one turns inward, casts out sense data and attains tranquility; after having accomplished this, one does not cling to objects of sense, but lives among them without being hindered by them. As Bunan, a seventeenth-century Rinzai master said, "While alive, become thoroughly dead, then do whatever you will, all is good." Similarly, as in Dongshan's famous line, "On a withered tree flowers bloom in a spring beyond time," the bequest of the great life after the great death is spoken of in many zen sayings and writings. Dogen said,

The great way of the buddhas is profound, wondrous, inconceivable; how could its practice be easy? Have you not seen how the ancients gave up their bodies and lives, abandoned their countries, cities, and families, looking upon them as like shards of tile? After that they passed eons living alone in the mountains and forests, bodies and minds like dead trees; only then did they unite with the way. Then they could use the mountains and rivers for words, raise the wind and rain for a tongue, and explain the great void, turning the incomparable wheel.

Thus it is not really a paradox when on one hand it is said one should be like wood or stone, yet it is also said one should not be like wood or stone. Baizhang spoke of the practical process in terms of three phases; "Just detach from all sound and form (etc.), and do not dwell in detachment, and do not dwell in intellectual understanding — this is practice." But as people are different and are not unified even as individuals, the application of this formula, as all zen formulae, depends on the person's condition: Baizhang said, "If you teach people only one phase, you'll make them go to hell; if you teach them all three phases at once, they'll go to hell by themselves."

Still, as Baizhang also points out, teaching of practice and realization is still not comprehensive; delusion and enlightenment are from the same source, and the way itself transcends this dualism. Ryusui said,

Emptiness is a name for nothingness, a name for ungraspibility, a name for mountains, rivers, the whole earth. It is also called the real form. In the green of the pines, the twist of the brambles, there is no going or coming; in the red of the flowers and the white of the snow there is no birth and no death. Joy, anger, love, pleasure — these are beginningless and endless; delusion, enlightenment, practice, realization — these are inexhaustible and boundless. Thus. Thus emptiness is the name for nothing else — all things are the real form, in all worlds in all directions there is no second, no third. Therefore, in the fundamental vehicle there is no delusion or enlightenment, no practice or realization — even to speak of practice and realization is a relative view; in our school from the first entry this point should be practiced whether sitting, lying down, or walking around. When sleeping, just sleeping, there's no past or future; when you awaken, there's no sleep either. This is called the absolute host.

TIMELESS SPRING

TRANSLATOR'S NOTE

Timeless Spring is an anthology of Chan-Zen writings and records illustrating diverse aspects of the rich and manysided teachings of Zen Buddhism. The selections presented here have been translated from the voluminous canon of Zen Buddhism, and trace manifestations of a major Zen teaching lineage over a period of nearly one thousand years in China and Japan. Sources for this anthology include the following Zen classics:

The Transmission of the Lamp
The Five Lamps Merged in the Source
Record of Further Inquiries
The Empty Valley Collection
The Vacant Hall Collection
Recorded Sayings of Hongzhi
Recorded Sayings of Rujing
Recorded Sayings of Dogen
Recorded Sayings of Geppa
Complete Works of Josai Daishi

Shitou said,

Our teaching has been handed down by the ancient buddhas; we do not speak of meditation or spiritual progress,
only the arrival at the knowledge and vision of buddhahood. Mind itself is buddha; mind, buddha, sentient beings, enlightenment, affliction, are all different names for
the same thing. You should know that your own mind's
aware essence is neither finite nor eternal, by nature
neither defiled nor pure. It is still and complete; it is the
same in ordinary people and saints, responding effectively
without patterns, apart from mind, intellect, and discriminating consciousness. The three realms — desire,
matter, and immaterial — and six states of being — animals, hell beings, hungry ghosts, titans, human beings,
gods — are only manifestations of your own mind; the
moon in the water, images in a mirror — how can there be
any birth or death? If you can realize this, you will be
complete in every way.

Once as Yaoshan was sitting, Shitou saw him and asked,
"What are you doing here?" Yaoshan said, "I'm not doing
anything." Shitou said, "Then you are just sitting idly."
Yaoshan said, "If I were idly sitting, that would be doing
something."

Shitou said, "You said you are not doing; what aren't
you doing?" Yaoshan said, "Even the saints don't know."

Merging of Difference and Unity

CAN TONG QI

Composed by Shitou Xiqian

> The mind of the great sage of India
> Is intimately communicated between east and west.[1]
> People's faculties may be keen or dull,
> But in the path there are no 'southern' or 'northern'
>   patriarchs.[2]
> The spiritual source shines clearly in the light;
> The branching streams flow in the darkness.[3]
> Grasping things is basically delusion;
> Merging with principle is still not enlightenment.
> Each sense and every field
> Interact and do not interact;
> When interacting, they also merge —
> Otherwise, they remain in their own states.
> Forms are basically different in material and
>   appearance,
> Sounds are fundamentally different in pleasant or
>   harsh quality.
> 'Darkness' is a word for merging upper and lower;
> 'Light' is an expression for distinguishing pure and
>   defiled.
> The four gross elements return to their own natures
> Like a baby taking to its mother;
> Fire heats, wind moves,
> Water wets, earth is solid.
> Eye and form, ear and sound;
> Nose and smell, tongue and taste —
> Thus in all things
> The leaves spread from the root;
> The whole process must return to the source;

'Noble' and 'base' are only manners of speaking.
Right in light there is darkness, but don't confront
*   it as darkness;*
Right in darkness there is light, but don't see it as
*   light.*[4]
Light and dark are relative to one another
Like forward and backward steps.
All things have their function —
It is a matter of use in the appropriate situation.
Phenomena exist like box and cover joining;
Principle accords like arrow points meeting.[5]
Hearing the words, you should understand the
*   source;*
Don't make up standards on your own.
If you don't understand the path as it meets your
*   eyes,*
How can you know the way as you walk?
Progress is not a matter of far or near,
But if you are confused, mountains and rivers block
*   the way.*
I humbly say to those who study the mystery,
Don't waste time.

NOTES TO CAN TONG QI

1. Commentators say that 'intimate' here does not mean secret, but that there is nothing hidden — this communication takes place everywhere, in everything.

2. The cliché about sudden chan of the south and gradual chan of the north in ancient China is probably well known to students of zen.

3. Light and dark are both 'turning words' used in both ways. Light can represent distinction, discriminating knowledge, life, etc.; then darkness represents merging, nondiscrimination, nirvana, etc. (there is more than one word in Chinese used to represent merging that is also semantically associated with darkness). In this respect Shitou is saying that the spiritual source, which is said to be like a quiet effulgence, is clear even in the midst of all sorts of distinctions and differences; these are all temporary,

existing relative to one another, ultimately equal in that what begins ends and the whole is going nowhere. Hence the 'branching streams' — the world of differentiation flows on in ultimate equanimity. One famous zen master explains that the spiritual source is mind, light is enlightenment, the branching streams are discriminating consciousnesses, and darkness is illusion; 'clearly seeing the purity of the mind, then knowledge suddenly appears, and in darkness becomes flowing consciousness, and passions arise.' (*Sandokai dokko, Tenkei rojin hoon shu 1*) These two interpretations say the same thing; unless the spiritual source and the branching streams fuse, one's supposed enlightenment is in fact partial; the heart of nirvana and the knowledge of differentiation are both essential to mastery of zen. If one clings to a state or quality of mind as a desired object and cannot function efficiently outside the conditions necessary to that state, a higher level of integration between the calm of nirvana and the experience and knowledge of the everyday world must be achieved. The primary motive force in this integration seems to be compassion.

4. We have discussed how merging, nondiscrimination, is a relative enlightenment; so this 'darkness' of unity should not be taken as darkness of insensibility; the emptiness in form is in the form itself, not an existing gap where no form exists. Hakuin said that the light of the mirror consciousness, the transformed storehouse consciousness, is 'pitch black' — if one abides by this as correct, he will be onesided and biased in his views. The knowledge of the objective world, though it cannot reasonably be overlooked, can never 'capture' anything outside the range of a limited receiving faculty and therefore could never be 'total' even before any abstract concerns arise. The terms 'sobriety' and 'intoxication' used by Sufi teachers are analogous to the zen terms light and darkness and are used as well on different levels, even plain meditation states.

5. Phenomena exist relative to one another, completing one another in terms seen as function, time, space, etc. This relativity is the principle itself; emptiness is figuratively described as the spaceless space which is the meeting point of two arrowheads. Two arrowheads meeting also connotes equivalence, equality; this sameness of reality is inherent in relative phenomena them-

selves — the principle cannot exist without the phenomena, even be it the phenomenon of the meditative state in which all sensation and perception disappear, symbolized by dying and seeing the way.

The commentaries consulted for this translation were Shigetsu's *Sandokai funogo,* Tenkei's *Sandokai dokko,* and *Sandokai katto shu* by Kishizawa Ian.

Song of the Jewel Mirror Awareness[1]

BAOJING SANMEIKE

Composed by Dongshan Liangjie

> *The teaching of thusness*
> *Has been intimately communicated by buddhas and*
>   *patriarchs;*
> *Now you have it,*
> *So keep it well.*
> *Filling a silver bowl with snow,*
> *Hiding a heron in the moonlight —*
> *When you array them, they're not the same;*
> *When you mix them, you know where they are.*[2]
> *The meaning is not in the words,*
> *Yet it responds to the inquiring impulse.*
> *If you're excited, it becomes a pitfall;*
> *If you miss it you fall into retrospective hesitation.*
> *Turning away and touching are both wrong,*
> *For it is like a mass of fire.*
> *Just to depict it in literary form*
> *Is to relegate it to defilement.*
> *It is bright just at midnight;*
> *It doesn't appear at dawn.*[3]
> *It acts as a guide for beings —*
> *Its use removes all pains.*

Although it is not fabricated,
It is not without speech.
It is like facing a jewel mirror;
Form and image behold each other —
You are not it
It actually is you.
It is like a babe in the world,
In five aspects complete;[4]
It does not go or come,
Nor rise nor stand.
"Baba wawa" —
Is there anything said or not?
Ultimately it does not apprehend anything,
Because its speech is not yet correct.[5]
It is like the six lines of the double split hexagram;
The relative and absolute integrate—
Piled up, they make three;
The complete transformation makes five.
It is like the taste of the five flavored herb,
Like the diamond thunderbolt.[6]
Subtly included within the true,
Inquiry and response come up together.
Communing with the source and communing with
        the process,
It includes integration and includes the road;
Merging is auspicious;
Do not violate it.[7]
Naturally real yet inconceivable,
It is not within the province of delusion or
        enlightenmennt.
With causal conditions, time and season,
Quiescently it shines bright.
In its fineness it fits into spacelessness;
In its greatness it is utterly beyond location.
A hairsbreadth's deviation
Will fail to accord with the proper attunement.
Now there are sudden and gradual,

In connection with which are set up basic
    approaches.
Once basic approaches are distinguished,
Then there are guiding rules.
But even though the basis is reached and the
    approach comprehended,
True eternity still flows.
Outwardly still while inwardly moving,
Like a tethered colt, a trapped rat —
The ancient saints pitied them,
And bestowed upon them the teaching;
According to their delusions,
They called black as white —
When erroneous imaginations cease,
The acquiescent mind realizes itself.
If you want to conform to the ancient way
Please observe the ancients of former times;
When about to fulfill the way of buddhahood,
One gazed at a tree for ten aeons,[8]
Like a tiger leaving part of its prey,
A horse with a white left hind leg.
Because there is the base, (there are)
Jewel pedestals, fine clothing;
Because there is the startlingly different, (there are)
House cat and cow.
Yi, with his archer's skill,
Could hit a target at a hundred paces;
But when arrowpoints meet head on,
What has this to do with the power of skill?[9]
When the wooden man begins to sing,
The stone woman gets up to dance;
It's not within reach of feeling or discrimination —
How could it admit of consideration in thought?
A minister serves the lord,
A son obeys the father.
Not obeying is not filial,
And not serving is no help.

Practice secretly, working within,
As though a fool, like an idiot —
If you can achieve continuity,
This is called the host within the host.

NOTES TO SONG OF
THE JEWEL MIRROR AWARENESS

1. Samadhi, concentration, meditation, trance, absorption, here we render awareness because of convenience, to avoid any suggestion of paranormality. The great Baizhang, with whom Dongshan's teacher Yunyan studied for twenty years, did not use the term samadhi for the mirror awareness, which he called the source, the king, the elixir of immortality; as long as it is not disturbed by anything in any circumstances, passing through all color and sound without lingering, it is the guide; yet he said one should not remain in the state of the mirror all the time. Though one must some time return to the source, it is still necessary, as Lopu said, to 'see the king in the busy marketplace.' In Dongshan's song, he speaks of this awareness sometimes as a medicinal trance, or simply basic awareness empty letting the flow through.

2. Silver and snow, herons and moonlight — all are white, yet not the same color. This symbolizes sameness and difference, and their interfusion. Sameness, symbolized by the common whiteness, is equality, equanimity, absence of ultimate reality; in relativity can be seen the merging of sameness and difference — without difference there can be no relation; in being dependent and conditional all are the same. Also this symbolizes absolute purity; when the mind is pure, all worlds are pure — this too is 'snow in a silver bowl'.

3. This means the same as the *Can Tong Qi*'s saying 'right in light there is darkness . . . right in darkness there is light.'

4. In the *Mahaparinirvanasutra* true thusness is likened to a baby in that it does not come or go, rise or stand and cannot speak.

Also this can mean complete with five senses, without conceptualization — this is the mirror trance. Ippen, the Japanese pure land saint, once said that the practice of invoking the name of the buddha to be reborn in the pure land affected the sixth consciousness; ending all discrimination of pure and impure, pleasant and painful, one realizes great bliss beyond extremes and sees the world as the field of the vow of the buddha of infinite light and life.

5. Baba wawa is to represent baby talk; the *Mahaparinirvanasutra* likens that which is materialized and that which is not — whatever is done becomes undone, and the whole process of doing in the infinite range of cosmoses cannot be described or compared, adequately conceived or thought. It is not doing anything because there is nothing to compare it to, nothing to indicate any direction.

6. The relative and absolute, or partial and true, are also called minister and ruler, son and father, light and darkness; Caoshan called the relative the world of myriad forms and the absolute the realm of emptiness; the relative is also called the phenomenal, and the absolute the principle. The relative within the absolute is realization of the emptiness of mind, whereby all things are emptied — thus it is the relative absolute containing the absolute relative. The absolute within the relative is the mirror awareness which is revealed by cleaning and polishing the mind by cessation and emptiness; at this point, the focus of concentration can make anything fill the universe, or make the universe into one point of awareness. Relative and absolute depend on each other, so two elements make three, adding their mutual intermingling, the source of the two. The absolute is always being expressed in the relative — this is the true absolute, but it is not always seen. Perfect comprehension of the relative grounded on experience of the absolute culminates in simultaneous realization of knowledge and complete peace and calm. At this point, Dongshan said, one 'comes back to sit among the ashes,' living this life as a wayfarer, expressing one's solidarity with the world in the vow to realize perfect enlightenment with all beings. The five flavored herb and diamond thunderbolt are images of five in one; these so-called ranks or positions, the set of five being the ultimate paradigm of dialectic and an illustration of meditational stages, are all from the same source, hence the association of five in one.

7. Dogen emphasized that practice and realization are not two separate things; the source and the process can be called absolute and relative as a device; integration and merging refer to these — this includes the road, or process itself, merging into the process, having no sense of seeking or acquisition, thus merging into the source. This was the point of the transcendance of wisdom scriptures.

8. Mahabhijnanabhibhu, an ancient buddha mentioned in the *Saddharmapundarika* or Lotus scripture, sat for ten aeons on the site of enlightenment, but did not realize perfect enlightenment or attain buddhahood, even though he sat with his body and mind perfectly still. Then gods from the heavens of the thirty three celestial kingdoms built a seat for him. When he sat on the seat, other gods and goddesses rained flowers around him for ten aeons, then still others played music for ten more eons. After ten aeons the buddha became enlightened and realized the truth. The scripture calls stillness and quiescence the ultimate nature of all things, but also an illusory citadel for those on the path to rest awhile, not an individual salvation because there is no self. The flowers and music represent the world of particulars, part of the sphere of knowledge of an omniscient buddha. Dongshan seems to use this old story with a slightly different emphasis; he recommends sitting for 'ten aeons' to make sure that there is no leaking of views, emotions, etc., when the celestial flowers begin to fall. This is consistent with the Cao-Dong saying emphasized by Dogen, 'eighty or ninety percent complete,' alluding to eternal bodhisattvahood, remaining in the causal state in this world to help deliver infinite beings to the other shore of the ocean of suffering, without craving personal liberation to the extent of willfully becoming totally extinct.

9. As seen in the *Can Tong Qi*, arrowpoints meeting symbolizes principle — mutual interdependence, absolute equality of dependent forces and entities. The lines before about the excellent and the inferior illustrate relativity. In buddhist science it is traditionally said that the workings of causes and effects are in fact inconceivable; we are in it, making conceptual models and devices to make use of what we can find out, but all of this is just a fragment of reality. In deep meditation one truly plunges into the unknown by not applying any way of knowing or seeing. The

meeting of arrowpoints also symbolizes the meeting of minds of teacher and disciple; regardless of what preparation went before, the actual meeting is not contrived, because it is the simple agreement of two minds seeing the same one reality.

(The sayings of Dongshan have been taken from *Dongshan yulu*; the commentaries consulted on the *Baojing sanmei ke* 'song of the jewel mirror awareness' are Tenkei's *Hokyozammai kimpei* and Shigetsu's *Hokyozammai funogo*.)

Sayings of Dongshan Liangjie

Dongshan asked a monk, "Where do you come from?" The monk said, "From a trip to a mountain." Dongshan said, "And did you reach the peak?" The monk said, "Yes." Dongshan said, "Was there anyone on the peak?" The monk said, "No." Dongshan said, "If so, you didn't reach the peak." The monk said, "If I didn't reach the peak, how could I know there was no one there?"

Dongshan said, "I had doubted this fellow."

When Xuefeng left Dongshan, Dongshan said, "Where are you going?" Xuefeng said, "I am going back into the ranges." Dongshan said, "By what way did you come out before?" Xuefeng said, "I came by way of flying monkey peak." Dongshan said, "Now that you are returning, which way will you go?" Xuefeng said, "I will go by way of flying monkey peak." Dongshan said, "There is someone who doesn't go by way of flying monkey peak; do you know him?" Xuefeng said, "No." Dongshan said, "Why don't you know him?" Xuefeng said, "He has no face." Dongshan said, "If you don't know him, how do you know he has no face?"

Xuefeng had no reply.

Once as Dongshan was eating some fruit with head monk Tai on a winter solstice day he asked, "There is one thing, which supports sky and earth; it is black as lacquer, and is always in the midst of activity, yet activity cannot contain it. Tell me, where is there fault?" Tai said, "The fault is in the activity."

Dongshan had an attendant take away the fruit tray.

Dongshan asked a monk, "What is your name?" The monk said it was so-and-so. Dongshan said, "Who is your master?" The monk said, "He is seen when replying." Dongshan said, "How miserable! People these days are all like this — they only recognize what's in front of an ass but behind a horse and take it to be their self. The decline of Buddhism is because of this. You don't even distinguish the host within the guest; how can you discern the host within the host?" The monk asked, "What is the host within the host?" Dongshan said, "Say it yourself." The monk said, "Even if I could say it, this would be the host within the guest — what is the host within the host?" Dongshan said, "It is easy to say this, but to continue is very hard."

Dongshan subsequently spoke a verse to the community, saying,

I regret to see followers of the way today
All stay by the gateway —
This is like heading for the imperial court
But stopping at an outlying pass.

Dongshan asked a monk, "What is the most miserable condition in the world?" The monk said, "Hell is most miserable." Dongshan said, "No. What is most miserable is to wear this robe without understanding the great matter."

Dongshan said to the community, "The late master Wuxie one day took a bath, burned incense, sat upright and said to the assembly, 'The body of reality is perfectly quiescent while giving the appearance of going and coming. The thousand sages are from the same source, myriad awarenesses are ultimately one. I am now a bubble bursting — what's the use of sadness? Don't trouble your minds; just maintain complete awareness. If you follow this order, you are really requiting my kindness — if you stubbornly go against what I say, you are not my disciples.' At that time a monk asked him, 'Where are you going?' Wuxie said, 'Nowhere.' The monk said, 'Why don't I see?' Wuxie said, 'It is not visible to the eye.'"

Dongshan added, "He was an adept."

Dongshan asked Yunju, "Where have you been?" Yunju said, "Walking in the mountains." Dongshan said, "Which mountain is suitable to live on?" Yunju said, "Which mountain is not suitable to live on?" Dongshan said, "Then you've checked out* all the mountains in the country?" Yunju said, "No." Dongshan said, "Then you've found an entry road." Yunju said, "There is no road." Dongshan said, "If there is no road, how can you meet me?" Yunju said, "If there were a road, then I would be a life apart** from you." Dongshan said, "Hereafter no one in the world will be able to pin you down."

Yunju built a hut on San peak. For days he didn't come to the monastery hall. Dongshan asked him, "Why haven't you come for meals recently?" Yunju said, "Every day a celestial spirit comes bringing an offering." Dongshan said, "I thought you were a real man, but you still entertain such a view. Come this evening."

---

*This word can also mean 'occupied'
**Some versions say (a) mountain(s) apart

Yunju came that evening; Dongshan called to him, "Hermit Ying!" Yunju responded; Dongshan said, "Don't think good, don't think bad — what is this?"

Yunju returned to his hut and sat completely quiet and still—hence the celestial spirit couldn't find him. After three days like this, it disappeared.

As Dongshan was traveling with Mi Shibo, they saw a vegetable leaf floating down a valley stream. Dongshan said, "If there were no one in the deep mountains, how could there be a vegetable leaf here? If we go upstream we might find a wayfarer staying there."

So they decided to make their way through the brush. After going several miles up the valley, suddenly they saw a strange looking emaciated figure of a man. It was master Longshan (Dragon Mountain), who was also known as Yinshan (Hidden Mountain or hidden in the mountains). They put down their packs and greeted him. Longshan said, "There is no road on this mountain — how did you get here?" Dongshan said, "Leaving aside the fact that there is no road, where did you enter?" Longshan said, "I didn't come by clouds or water." Dongshan said, "How long have you been living on this mountain?" Longshan said, "The passing of seasons and years cannot reach it." Dongshan said, "Were you here first or was the mountain here first?" Longshan said, "I don't know." Dongshan said, "Why not?" Longshan said, "I don't come from celestial or human realms." Dongshan said, "What truth have you realized that you come to dwell here on this mountain?" Longshan said, "I saw two clay bulls fighting go into the ocean and up till now have no news of them."

Now for the first time Dongshan bowed with full respect for Longshan. Then he asked, "What is the guest within the host?" Longshan said, "The blue mountain is covered by white clouds." Dongshan said, "What is the host within the host?" Longshan said, "He never goes out the door." Dongshan asked, "How far apart are host and guest?" Longshan said, "Waves on a river." Dongshan said, "When guest and host meet, what is said?" Longshan said, "The pure breeze sweeps the white moon." Dongshan took his leave and departed.

DONGSHAN'S SELF-ADMONITION

Don't seek fame or profit, glory or prosperity. Just pass this life as is, according to conditions. When the breath vanishes, who is the master? After the death of the body, there is only an empty name. When your clothes are worn out, repair them over and over; when you've no food, work to provide. How long can an illusory body last? For its idle concerns would you increase your ignorance?

DONGSHAN'S GUIDELINES

Buddhist ascetics make the lofty their source; having cut off clinging ties, you should go the way of simplicity and poverty. Cut off gratitude and love for your father and mother, abandon the formalities of sovereign and subject. Shave your hair, dye your clothing; taking the cloth and carrying the bowl, tread the shortest way out of the dusts and climb the stairway into sainthood.* Pure as frost,

*This passage refers to leaving family and society and becoming a monk or nun; shaven heads and black clothing are emblematic of renunciation, and the cloth and bowl are among the few implements considered sufficient for renunciants. The Japanese zen master Dogen, who always praised Dongshan highly, had a great deal to say on the practical ideals of the renunciate life, and followed it himself most of his life.

clean as snow, dragons and spirits will honor you, ghosts and sprites will submit to you.

Concentrate singlemindedly; when you requite the profound debt of gratitude to the buddhas, only then will the body born of your parents be saved. How could it be permissible to form a cult, gather followers and associates, take up pen and ink and dash off compositions, toil in pursuit of dust for love of fame and profit, neglect the rules of ethics and destroy proper conduct? Grasping one lifetime of ease becomes myriad aeons of pain; if you develop like this, you are calling yourselves buddhists in vain.

Caoshan
on the Five Ranks

Caoshan Benji met Donghsan Liàngjie near the end of the latter's life, and is said to have received from him the esoteric teaching of the Baojingsanmei and the five ranks or positions of the absolute and relative together, later elaborated with a variety of symbolic pairs. The records of Caoshan and Dongshan seem to have existed in a scattered state for some time and were collected as known today in late medieval Japan; some of the sayings of Caoshan seem to have been attributed also to the second, possibly even third generation Caoshan. Benji was known as Caoshan the former and it was in his school that the five ranks were most elaborated in the early Cao-Dong lineage. The following are some of Caoshan's descriptions of the five ranks of absolute and relative.

COMING FROM WITHIN THE ABSOLUTE

The whole body revealed, unique; the root source of all things, in it there is neither praise nor blame.

ARRIVING WITHIN THE RELATIVE

Going along with things and beings without hindrance, a wooden boat empty inside, getting through freely by being empty.

THE RELATIVE WITHIN THE ABSOLUTE

A piece of emptiness pervading everywhere, all senses silent.

THE ABSOLUTE WITHIN THE RELATIVE

The moon in the water, the image in the mirror — fundamentally without origin or extinction, how could any traces remain.

ARRIVAL IN BOTH AT ONCE

The absolute is not necessarily void, the relative is not necessary actual; there is neither turning away nor turning to.

When mental activity sinks away and both the material world and emptiness are forgotten, there is no more concealment — the whole thing is revealed; this is the relative within the absolute.

Mountains are mountains, rivers are rivers — no one establishes the names, nothing can be compared; this is the absolute within the relative.

51

Clean and naked, bare and free, the visage is in full majesty — throughout all heaven and earth, the sole honored one, without any other; this is coming from the absolute.

Just as the emperor in his realm does not rely upon the ordinances of wise kings and emperors of the past, the eye sees and the ear hears without using any other power.

As the ear does not enter sound, and sound does not block up the ear, the moment you turn therein, there have never been any names fixed in the world. This is called arrival within both at once. This is not mind or objects, not phenomena or principle; it has always been beyond name or description. Naturally real, forgetting essence and appearance, this is called simultaneous realization of both relative and absolute.

Caoshan used terms and images borrowed from ancient Chinese books as well. The five ranks have cosmic as well as meditative and 'metaphysical' implications. The so-called five ranks of accomplishment are slightly different and are all subsumed within the relative until the ultimate point when there is complete integration. The great Rinzai master Hakuin said that there was a great deal of confusion surrounding the five ranks; this teaching can be a useful tool or a swirling vortex.

The Three Falls of Caoshan

The following notes are extracts from the laconic sayings of Caoshan about what he called three 'falls.' Their original form is not known, and here we have taken different sayings from different conversations and put them all together under the fall to which they refer.

THE FALL OF ASCETICS

Being a buffalo, wearing hair and horns; not clinging to the business of asceticism or the states of reward of saints. Not staying in the absolute, not choosing one's estate.

THE FALL OF THE PRECIOUS

Not enjoying food; this ('food') is the fundamental endowment; knowing it exists yet not grasping it is called the fall of the precious. The body of reality, objective reality, are precious things; they too must be overturned — this is the fall of the precious. For example, the White Ox on Open Ground is the ultimate symbol of the body of reality; this too must be overturned so as to avoid settling down in uniformity without discernment.

THE FALL ACCORDING TO KIND

Not cutting off sound and form. As a beginner, knowing there is one's own fundamental endowment; then turning back the light, shutting out all form, sound, smell, taste, feeling and conception, to attain tranquility. Then, after fully accomplishing this, not clinging to the six sense fields, 'falling' into them without being befuddled, letting be, unhindered. Ordinary feelings and religious experiences ended and forgotten, no more need to cut off anything in the fields of sense experience; then you can take 'food.'

The fundamental endowment, also called 'one's own thing' as well as 'that man' and 'the original face,' is often spoken of in Cao-Dong chan; that is what they want us to know exists to begin with. Nanquan Puyuan, one of the ancients with whom Dongshan once studied, said, 'First go over to the other side and realize it exists; then come back to this side to practice.'

Caoshan said,

Yunmen asked Caoshan, "Will you receive someone who does not change?" Caoshan said, "I have no such leisure."

A monk raised the question of the officer Luxuan to Nanquan, "What is your surname?" Nanquan said, "Wang (King)." Luxuan said, "Does the 'king' have retainers?" Nanquan said, "The four ministers are not ignorant." Luxuan said, "What position does the king occupy?" Nanquan said, "Moss grows in the jade palace." The monk asked Caoshan, "What does it mean, that 'moss grows in the jade palace'?" Caoshan said, "He does not dwell in the absolute state." The monk asked, "What happens when they come to court from the eight directions?" Caoshan said, "He does not receive their homage." The monk asked, "Then what's the use of coming to court?" Caoshan said, "Any who disobey are killed." The monk said, "Disobedience is on the part of the minister; what about the position of the lord?" Caoshan said, "Even the private councillor doesn't get the message." The monk said, "Then the accomplishment of harmony and order rests with the ministers." Caoshan said, "Do you know the meaning of the lord?" The monk said, "One on the outside dare not try to assess it."

A monk asked, "How is it when the five ranks face a guest?" Caoshan said, "What state are you asking about right now?" The monk said, "I am coming from the relative state; I ask you to receive me in the absolute state." Caoshan said, "No." The monk said, "Why not?" Caoshan said, "It might fall into the relative."

Caoshan then asked the monk back, "Is this not receiving dealing with the guest or not?" The monk said, "It is already dealing with the guest." Caoshan said, "Right."

Sayings of Yunju

Chan master Daoying of Yunju monastery in Hong prefecture was a man from Yudian in Yu prefecture; his lay surname was Wang.

When he was a child he followed a teacher and received instruction. At the age of twenty five he was fully ordained at the Yanshou monastery in Fanyang. His original teacher made him study the collection of writings for buddhist disciples (books of ancient buddhism). He sighed and said, "Why should a healthy man be fettered by rules of discipline?" So he went and called on Suiwei to inquire about the way. He passed three years there.

A certain cloud-wandering monk came from Yuzhang, profusely extolling the meditation school of the chan master Dongshan Liangjie. Then Daoying went there; Dongshan asked him, "What is your name?" He replied, "Daoying." Dongshan said, "Say beyond this." He said, "If I were to say beyond this, I would not name it Daoying." Dongshan said, "No difference from my reply to Yunyan."

Later Yunju asked, "What is the intent of the patriarchs?" Dongshan said, "Later when you have a thatch roof over your head and suddenly someone asks you, how will you answer?" Yunju said, "I am at fault."

One time Dongshan said to Yunju, "I heard that master Sida was born in the land of Japan and became a king; is that true or false?" Yunju said, "If it were Sida, he wouldn't even become a buddha, much less a king." Dongshan agreed with this.

Dongshan said to Yunju, "In the past Nanquan questioned a monk who was lecturing on the scripture about the birth of the future buddha Maitreya, the loving one; 'When is Maitreya going to come down to be born here?' The monk said, 'Now he is in heaven; in the future he will come down to be born.' Nanquan said, 'There is no Maitreya in heaven; there is no Maitreya on earth.'"

As Yunju heard this recitation he asked, "About this 'there is no Maitreya in heaven or on earth,' who gives the names?" Dongshan's meditation seat rocked; "Reverend Ying!" he said.

Dongshan asked, "The great incorrigible* kills his father and mother, sheds buddha's blood and disrupts the harmonious community; in these various deeds where is filial care?" Yunju said, "Only these are real filial care." From this point on Dongshan approved of Yunju and made him the leader in the room (inner circle).

One day Yunju went up into the hall and quoted Dongshan's old saying, "Hell is not really painful; wearing this vestment, to fail to understand the great matter, that loss is most painful." The master Yunju then said to the assembly, "You are already within this tradition; a hundred percent is not far from ninety percent; you should exert a little more energy. Then you elders will not tire of your perpetual journey and yet will not turn away from the monastery. An ancient said, 'If you wish to be able to bear this matter, you must go stand atop the highest mountain, and walk on the bottom of the deepest sea. Only then have you some power.' If you have not yet taken care of the great matter, for now you must tread the hidden road."

Someone asked, "What is esteemed by an ascetic?"

Yunju said, "Where mind's consciousness does not reach."

*Great incorrigible is another name for a bodhisattva, who always stays in the world, is never 'saved.' Father and mother symbolize ignorance and lust; shedding buddha's blood symbolizes plunging into the mindless, thoughtless, formless state; disrupting the community symbolizes realizing that all afflictions and passions and compulsions are empty and baseless.

Someone asked, "What are the grades of buddhas and patriarchs?"

Yunju said, "Both are grades."

Someone asked, "What is the meaning of the coming of Bodhidharma from the west?"

Yunju said, "Meeting no one on the ancient road."

Yunju taught for over thirty years and had twenty-eight enlightened disciples before he died in 902. It was Daoying's succession that lasted in China and Japan, while the transmission lines of Caoshan, Sushan, Qinglin, and Dongshan's other great disciples died out after several generations. The foregoing excerpts are taken from the biography of Yunju Daoying in the *Jingte chuan deng lu,* a classic chan history in which Yunju is listed as the first of Dongshan's heirs.

After the deaths of Dongshan's great disciples and their heirs, with the eventual return of several teaching lines to inactivity, fewer new teachers succeeded in realizing and transmitting enlightenment. This is a general trend in chan and other forms of buddhism as well as worldly affairs after the passing of great teachers and exemplars.

In the fifth through eighth generation of the Dongshan succession there was something of a revival, with the appearance of several distinguished chan masters. There are several collections of kungan, ancient chan stories, along with commentaries in verse and prose, which were products of distinguished leaders of Caodong chan practice during and after this revival. At this point the so-called schools of chan were mixed and fully recognized one another because it is not a fabricated teaching, but there were traditional forms of expression and technique as well as innovations having nothing to do with any school as such. Followers and enthusiasts, however, were talking volubly about the styles of different sects of chan. In the eleventh century the Caodong, Linji, and Yunmen were greatly thriving.

In the eighth generation of the Dong succession there appeared the great chan master Furong Daokai (1042-1118), who was famous in the monasteries for his lofty practice of the way. The governor of the capital city petitioned the emperor to honor him so as to elevate his example; Daokai refused the honor, however, on the grounds that when he had left home to seek enlightenment in his youth he promised his parents that he would not do anything for gain or honor, but only investigate the way in all sincerity. It was because of this that his parents allowed him to leave home and abandon society; now the emperor had him banished to southeast China for going against the imperial will for refusing the title and piece of purple vestment that had been bestowed on him officially. Later he was allowed to settle on Mt. Furong (lotus mountain) in Fukien, where many ascetics had practiced meditation and buddhist communities had long existed. Here many people came to him and his teaching was widely reknowned. The following excerpts of his sayings are taken from *Wudeng Huiyuan 14.*

Furong said,

Going into the Jeta Grove by day, the bright moon is in the sky; climbing Vulture Peak* by night, the sun fills the eyes. The raven is like snow; lone geese form a flock. An iron dog howls through the night, fighting clay bulls go into the sea — at this time, all everywhere are gathered together; what difference is there between others and self? On the terrace of the ancient buddhas, in the house of the patriarchs, everybody puts forth a hand to greet the friends who come and go. But tell me, good people, what does this amount to? (a long silence) Plant more shadowless trees for people of later times to see.

As soon as I get up on the seat to speak, I am already involved in the dusts — if I go on and freeze my eyes, it would just show a flaw. The special transmission in a

*Jeta Grove and Vulture Peak were famous places where Shakyamuni Buddha taught.

single statement is taking in a thief who ransacks your house; not losing the fundamental source is like a fox fond of its den. Therefore true thusness, ordinary and holy, is all dream talk; buddhas and sentient beings are expressions of assumptions. When you get here turn the light around to shine back, let go your hands and accept it — even then you still will not have escaped being like a cold cicada clinging to a dead tree, not turning his head when his crying ends.

He raised his staff and said,

If you can get it here, it is all something set up by the buddhas. Even if you can spring up in the east and disappear in the west, open out or shut away freely, you still haven't even dreamed of seeing what was before the buddhas. You should know that there is one man who doesn't get anything from others, does not accept any teaching or command, and does not fall within the scope of grade or rank. If you know this man, your life's study is completed. (Suddenly he called out to the assembly and said,) If you freeze your eyes any more, don't bother to see me.

When using words to tell about the path, we are limited to the present time; even if a tongueless man can speak and a legless man can walk, still they cannot merge with 'that man' (mentioned before). Do you understand? When the dragon howls, it's pointless to turn an ear to it; when the tiger roars, it's vain to sink into thought.

Someone asked, "What are words expressing mutual integration?" He replied, "The inconceivable function, wholly employed, encompasses the world; a wooden man strolls through the fire."

STANDARDS OF JETAVANA

The following speech was given on Mt. Furong

Those who leave home and society do so because they are
fed up with mundane turmoil and seek liberation from
birth and death. Therefore they rest their minds and stop
their thoughts, cutting off clinging involvements; that is
why they are called renunciants. How can we bury our
daily lives away for gain and honor? You must let go of
both sides and cast down the middle, being in the midst
of sound and form like flowers planted on rock, seeing
profit and fame as dust in the eye. Still it is not that it
hasn't been happening since beginningless time, or that
we are ignorant of the process, but it is making the head
into the tail; why should you suffer so for your greedy attachment in such a situation? If you don't stop now, when
are you waiting for? This is why ancient sages taught
people to be complete in the present; if you can be complete in the present, what else is there? If you can get to
have nothing on your mind, even the buddhas and enlightened ancestors are enemies — all mundane things will
naturally be cool and simple. Then for the first time you
merge with the other side.

Have you not read how Yinshan (Longshan) would
never see people, how Zhaozhou would never ask of
people — they gathered loads of chestnuts for food. Damei
wore lotus leaves; the Paper-robed Wayfarer just wore paper, and Elder Xuantai only wore muslin. Shishuang set
up a 'dead tree hall' and sat and reclined along with the
others* — he only wanted your mind to die. Touzi had
people prepare rice, cooked it with them and ate together
with them—he wanted insight into what you're about.
Now since ancient times there have been such examples of

*According to the *Jiungde Chuandeng lu,* Shishuang's community
never lay down, always sat—that is why they were called the
dead tree congregation.

the sages. If they had no worth, how could they be endured? Good people, if you can see this through here, you will surely not cheat anybody; but if you do not agree to take this up, I fear you will waste effort later.

It is my practice not to take from or add to a monastery; how could I sit around wasting the community property and abruptly forget the bequest of past sages? Now I am following the example of the ancients in acting as abbot; together with you all we have decided not to go down the mountain any more, not to go to feasts, not to send preachers to collect contributions, but just take account of what this monastery's lands produce and divide it into three hundred and sixty equal parts, using one part each day, not increasing or decreasing according to people. If there's enough rice, then make cooked rice; if not enough for rice, make gruel; if there is not enough for gruel, we'll make rice water. New arrivals for interviews will be given hot water only; no snack will be given. Only one tea hall will be set up. Take care of your tasks by yourself — the essential thing is to cut down on entanglements and concentrate wholly on comprehending the way.

Especially when subsistence is ample, the scenery luxurious, the flowers can bloom, the birds can sing; the wooden horse neighs forever, the stone ox gallops, the blue mountains beyond the skies are pale, the gurgling stream by the ear has no sound. Up in the mountains monkeys howl as the dew soaks the midnight moon; in the woods the cranes whoop as the wind returns to the dawn pines.

When the spring wind rises, in a dead tree a dragon murmurs. When the autumn leaves wither and fall, flowers scatter in the cold forest. The jade stairway is spread with moss designs, the people's faces are tinged with smoke and haze. The sound and dust is stilled, all events are the same — one flavor, solitary, there is no way to approach.

Now as I've told about my household in front of everyone, I have ready slipped; why should I go on to lecture in the hall, have interviews in the room, raise my gavel and whisk, shout here and beat there, raise my eyebrows and glare my eyes like a lunatic? I would not only bog you elders down, but I would also go against the sages of former times.

Have you not heard how Bodhidharma came from the West and sat facing a wall for nine years on Shaoshi mountain, the second patriarch came and stood in the snow, and cut off his arm — one could say they fully experienced hardship and pain. But Bodhidharma never said a word and the second patriarch didn't ask anything — can you say Bodhidharma didn't help the man? Can you say the second patriarch did not seek a teacher?

Whenever I get down to speaking of what the ancient sages did, I feel there is no place to put my body — it is shameful how soft and weak people of later generations are, especially when you provide each other with delicious feasts, saying, "We can set our resolve only when we have enough food, clothing, medicine, and bedding." I am just afraid you'll put your hands and feet out of coordination and be lives away. Time is swift as an arrow — one should be very careful of how it is used. Even so, it still is a matter for other people, to figure out together in good time; I cannot teach you by force. Haven't you heard this ancient verse —

> Mountain fields yield millet and rice
> Wild vegetables and thin yellow soup —
> Eat if you want;
> If you don't eat, go where you will.

I only hope people on the same path will each work hard on their own. Take care.

Danxia said,

Danxia was a successor of Furong Daojie. *Wudeng Huiyuan 14*

"Within heaven and earth, in the universe, there is a jewel hidden in the mountain of form." In speaking this way, Sengzhao, master of the teachings, only knew how to point to its traces and talk about its tracks; but he didn't know how to bring it out to show it to people. Today I will break open the universe, shatter the mountain of form, and bring it out for you. Those who have eyes should discern it. (he set his staff up) Do you see? When a heron stands in the snow they are not the same color; the bright moon and the white reed flowers are not identical.

Deshan said to his community, "My school has no sayings — really there is nothing to give people." Deshan's speaking like this could be called only knowing how to go into the weeds to look for people without being aware of getting his whole body soaked in mud and water. If you examine closely, he only has one eye. As for me, I am otherwise. My school has a saying, with a profound and mysterious message which a golden knife could not cut open — a jade woman becomes pregnant by night.

Sayings of
Changlu Zhenxie Qingliao

Danxia Zichun asked him, "What is the self before the empty aeon?" As Changlu was about to reply, Danxia said, "You're still noisy — go away for now."

One day as he climbed Bowl Peak his mind opened up into enlightenment. He took a short cut down and went back to stand by Danxia, who slapped him and said, "I thought you knew it exists." Changlu bowed joyfully.

The next day Danxia went into the hall and said, "The sun illumines the green of the solitary peak; the moon shines in the cold of the valley stream. Don't put the wondrous secret of the ancestral teachers in your little heart." Then he got off the seat. Changlu came directly forward and said, "Your address today can't fool me any more." Danxia said, "Try to recite my address." Changlu remained silent. Danxia said, "I thought you had a glimpse." Changlu then left.

Later, at Gaoning monastery, Changlu said, "At my late master's slap my abilities were exhausted and I couldn't find a way to open my mouth."

Crossing a log bridge on a solitary peak, even if you go right ahead like this, this is still where people's feet are high and low. If you see all the way through, you reach everywhere without going out the door; without ever going in the door you are always in the room. Otherwise, if you are not yet thus, haul some firewood for the cold.

If you can say the first statement, you will not be fooled by the staff. If you know the staff, this is still a matter of the road. What is the statement of arriving at the destination?

You look everywhere without finding, but there is a place where you find spontaneously without looking. But tell me, what place is that? (a long silence) The thief's body is already showing.

When white mold grows around your mouth,* you first gain entry into the door; when your whole body is inflamed,* then you know there is something inside. You should also know that there is one who doesn't go out the door. What do you call a door?

A monk asked, "the buddhas of past, present, and future turn the great wheel of Dharma in flames of fire — is it correct or not?" Changlu said laughing, "I have doubts, after all." The monk asked, "Why do you doubt?" Changlu said, "The fragrance of wildflowers fills the pathways, but the hidden birds don't know it's spring."

Is there anyone who is not defiled by mystic wonder? (a long silence) This one spot could not be washed away even if you dumped the waters of the oceans on it.

From *Wudeng Huiyuan 14*

*White mold growing around the mouth means silence, non-doing. A monk asked Yaoshan, 'How is it when a student wants to return home?' Yaoshan said, 'Your parents' whole bodies are inflamed, lying in a forest of thorns; where will you return?' The monk said, 'Then I won't go back.' Yaoshan said, 'You should return! If you return home, I'll tell you a way to end the need for provisions.' The monk said, 'Please tell me.' Yaoshan said, 'At mealtimes, don't chew through even a grain of rice.' The white mold and inflamed body signify total detachment, then subsistence in the world as is, yet free from greed (not 'chewing through').

Hongzhi said,

Hongzhi was also a disciple and heir of Danxia Zichun, and became one of the most famous Cao-Dong chan masters of all time; a great poet and eloquent speaker, he left a rich teaching, preserved by his disciples. The following excerpts are from a collection of Hongzhi's sayings and writings.

All things originate from the mind. When the whole mind is silent, all appearances end. Which is other, which is self? Because at this time there is no sign of differentiation, not even a single atom can be established. When not a single thought is born, you penetrate through before the womb and after the skin bag; one point of inconceivable illumination, whole and undifferentiated, without corners, edge or traces, this cannot be dimmed; what cannot be dimmed is called inherent knowledge. But the point of inherent knowledge is called the fundamental endowment — after all there is nothing whatever gotten beyond one's lot. Empty, open, subtly aware without any images, really hearing without echoes. Thus it is said, "It is not within reach of eye and ear." This is the ultimate point of reaching mystic accord. Light emanates from there and the universe is reflected everywhere in this — everything is it. All are states experienced alone by patchrobed monks. But essentially we don't borrow some else's household things; it is absolutely necessary to clearly realize it personally. Seedlings of my house must be like this.

When you realize all things are empty, then you are free in all states of mind and penetrate beyond through every atom of dust. The primordial beam of light pervades everywhere, and then transforms according to the energies and situations; everything it meets is the source — subtly illumining all things, empty and without partner; the wind in the pines, the moon in the water — clear harmony, with no wandering mind, no sticking to appearances. The essence lies in being empty inside and having free space, responding outwardly without getting mixed up, like spring bearing flowers, like a mirror reflecting images; in the midst of floods of tumult you will naturally stand serene above it all.

Where your state is thoroughly peaceful and your livelihood is cool and serene, then you will see the emptiness of the ages; there is nothing to be troubled with, nothing that can obstruct. Empty, absolute and radiant, clear, complete and shining — it clearly exists for all ages, never dimmed. If you know the thing here with a nod of the head, you do not follow birth and death or abide in annihilation or eternity. When you want to make an appropriate change, then you transform along with the myriad forms of the multitude of appearances. If you want to remain tranquil, then you cover and uphold in the same way as sky and earth — appearing or disappearing, shutting down or opening up, all are up to you.

Seeing the sun by day and the moon by night — the time when there is no deception is where a patchrobed monk walks steady in peace — naturally there are no corners or seams. If you want to be this even and peaceful, you must put an end to the subtle pounding and weaving in the mind. Do you want to not grumble? You must cut it off ('sit through it') and cast it down. Then you can shine through it all. Light and reflection are both forgotten, skin and flesh fallen off; all senses totally purified, naturally the eyes are clear. Your resources are fully complete, you don't get hung up anywhere, but are in harmony at all times. Right in illumination there is darkness, right in darkness there is illumination. A solitary boat carries the moon; at night it rests in the reed flowers. The one beam of light is after all like this.

Clean, pure, perfectly clear; the power of the eye cannot reach its bounds. Still, silent, empty and vast — the ken of the mind cannot find its edges. One who investigates sincerely and really arrives considers this his fundamental ground; neither buddhas nor demons can enter, dust or dirt cannot defile it. It fits in square or round, its course of action is exactly appropriate. Then infinities of inconceivable functions, complementing each other subtly, spring forth from this ground and come to an end in this ground. Everybody has what is there.

There is utterly no way to study this matter; the essence lies in emptying and opening body and mind so they are vast as space, then you will naturally be complete everywhere. This awareness cannot be dimmed, this clarity cannot be mixed up. The moon follows the flowing waters, the rain goes with the moving clouds. Ultimately there are not so many minds that can produce so many things — just do not hinder things by yourself, and naturally nothing will hinder you. Body and mind one suchness, there is nothing outside the body. The same substance, the same function, one essence, one character. Each and every sense and sensation is immediate and absolute. Therefore it was said that a saint has no self, but there is nothing that is not himself. It is so obvious, so clear; then you realize that gathered in or let out it has become a white bull on open ground, which you cannot drive away even if you try.*

The action and repose of people of the way is like flowing clouds without mind, like the full moon reflecting everywhere. They are not stopped by anything — clearly in the midst of myriad forms, they stand out serene. In contact with the course of circumstances, they are not affected or mixed up, having the same function as those which have the same substance as themselves. Words cannot communicate this, thought cannot reach it. Transcen-

*The white bull symbolizes the body of reality; its whiteness symbolizes equality, uniformity. The open ground is true thusness. The discipline of raising the bull is to expand a spot of clear awareness to cover the world.

dent, absolute, free, beyond effort, it is realized inconceivably outside of intellection and emotion. It is put to use on the road, taken up at home; comprehending birth and death, going beyond cause and condition, real vision is the quality of awareness and fundamentally has no abode. This is why it is said, "The all-pervading mind does not abide anywhere."

When you stop and rest, it is like the ocean taking in the hundred rivers — all come here to one flavor. When you let go and act, it is like the eternal tide riding the rushing wind — it all comes here going along together. Is this not arriving at the real source, attaining manifestation of the great function? Patchrobed monks change appropriately according to the situation — they should be like this. But when did you ever establish your mind and think up material circumstances? You must comprehend this thoroughly.

Walking in the void, forgetting conditions, shining through beyond the shadows, one point of spirituality radiant and undimmed. The mind of past, present, and future is cut off, the entanglements of the gross elements ended. Empty and clear, wondrously bright, shining alone through the ages; when patchrobed monks can be like this, then they are not bound by birth and death. As they act, they let go over the cliff, with nothing to hold on to; the thread under their feet cut off, they totally transcend in one step. The buddhas and patriarchs do not tread one's own real and true wondrously shining ground; this is called oneself — this is the time when one inherits the family business. As soon as you get involved in thought, you get stuck in the flow of routine. Empty, always aware; clear, yet always shining — the whiteness of the reed flowers and clarity of the bright moon merge; rowing in a solitary boat, blowing free, untrammelled — this time is where it's at. But tell me, who is this? Look quickly to determine.

A patchrobed monk wandering through the world

should empty and open his mind, so there is not a speck of dust therein. Only then can he respond skillfully, not be impeded by things, and not be bound by principles — fully appearing and disappearing therein, he has his share of freedom; as soon as one gets involved in intellectual thoughts, one is buried. The essence is to embody it fully — then naturally the wandering sword and myriad states neither clash or avoid each other; the box and lid meet perfectly. Able to gather in from outside and cut off all flowing leaks, this is called a fellow who can manage the family business. After all he comes back from here; the white clouds enter the valley, the bright moon circles the mountains — there is a time when one merges with the 'father.' That is why it is said, "Three people lean on one staff and sleep on one bed."* Inside and out there are no traces at all — merged into one whole, free as clouds of mist and rain, deep as the waters of dewy autumn. Good people, you must remember this thing before you can attain realization.

Empty, vacant, clear, quiet; cool, austere, pure, real — in this way are cleared up residual habits of many lives. When the defilement of remaining habits is ended, the original light appears, shining through your skull. It does not admit anything else; clear and open, it is like sky and water merging in autumn, like the snow and moon having the same color. This realm has no boundaries; it is beyond location. Vast and solid, without edges or seams, you must still slough off everything completely here before you will realize. When you have sloughed off everything, thought and speech are thousands of miles away; there is no discerning principle — so how could there be anything to

---

*This means that real communication takes place by forgetting self and merging with one reality. By forgetting self and others one merges with the one reality. As noted before, 'father' is a symbol for absolute reality as well as ignorance.

point out anymore? Only one whose bucket's bottom has fallen out will believe completely. That is why it is said, "Just realize union; when union is realized you can spring into action and enter the world." The attainment of freedom of action will be clearly evident. Sound and form, shadow and echo, are immediate, without traces.

Public Cases from the Record of Further Inquiries

CASE

Baqiao said to the assembly, "If you have a staff, I'll give you the staff; if you have no staff, I'll take your staff away."

Tiantong Hongzhi brought this up and said, "If you have, then all have; if you have not, all have not. Having or not only depends on the person concerned; is giving or taking away any business of Baqiao? At this moment, what about your staff?"

Wansong comments, "Chan master Huiqing of Baqiao Mountain in Ying province succeeded to Guangyong of the Southern Stupa, who succeeded to Yangshan; so Baqiao was a great-grandson of Guishan. In a talk in the hall, he said, 'When I was twenty-eight I came to Mt. Yang and saw the master of the southern stupa there (Guangyong) go up into the hall and say, "You people, if you are the real thing, you would know how to roar like a lion the moment you're born from your mother's womb — wouldn't that be delightful?" At that time, at his words, I set body and mind to rest, and stayed there for five years.'

"Baqiao said to his group, 'If you have a staff, I'll give you the staff.' I say, the patriarchal teacher didn't come from the West, to transmit a wonderful secret at Shaolin; what's the need for Bodhidharma to point directly to the human mind? Baqiao also said, 'If you have no staff, I'll take your staff away.' Even if you don't bring along even a single thing, yet you must even cast that off before you will attain realization.

"Master Che of Dagui said, 'I am not so; if you have a staff, I will take your staff away; if you have no staff, I will give you a staff. As Dagui is like this, can you people use it or not? If you can't use it, then for the time being return it to the original owner.' I say, he poles the boat along with the flow; people of the time know it exists.

"Tiantong brought this out — for a great man, having or not rests with oneself; it is not subject to Baqiao's judgement and disposition. This has since time immemorial been called the staff of a patchrobed monk. Tiantong feared that the person responsible would avoid it, so he said further, 'At this moment, what about your staff?' Even if you can bring it out, don't let me see it, or I'll break it into eight pieces, burn it up and let the ashes blow away. I am old — it's all right to keep it too. Why? Sometimes it helps one across a river where the bridge is broken; how many times has it accompanied me back to the moonlit village?"

CASE

When Yantou took leave of Deshan, Deshan said, "Where are you going?" Yantou said, "For now I'm taking leave of you, Master, and going down the mountain." Deshan said, "After that, then what?" Yantou said, "I won't forget you, master." Deshan said, "By virtue of what do you say this?" Yantou said, "Haven't you heard that when one's knowledge is equal to his teacher's, he has less than half his teacher's virtue; when one's knowledge surpasses the teacher's, only then is he qualified for the transmission." Deshan said, "So it is. So it is. Guard it well on your own."

Tiantong Hongzhi brought this up and said, "Deshan usually did not set up buddhas or patriarchs under his cane, but here, in this situation, he was so kind. Even though this is sustenance for an adopted son, how can he avoid getting criticism from people of later times? When (Yantou) said, 'When one's knowledge surpasses the teacher, only then is he qualified for the transmission,' I would drag out a staff and hit him right across the back."

Wansong comments, "Chan master Yantou Quanhuo, when he first called on Deshan, carried his sitting mat up into the hall and looked up at Deshan, who saw him and said, 'What are you doing?' Yantou scolded him; Deshan said, 'Where is my fault?' Yantou said, 'A double case,' then went down to meditate in the hall. Deshan thought to himself, 'This monk somewhat resembles a pilgrim.' So at the end, when he took leave of Deshan, Deshan said, 'Where are you going?' and Yantou said, 'For now I'm leaving you and going down the mountain.' Deshan said, 'After that, then what?' Yantou said, 'I won't forget you, master.' All of this is proper to teacher and apprentice, no different from anywhere else. Deshan also asked, 'Based on what do you say this?' Yantou said, 'Haven't you heard that when one's knowledge is equal to his teacher, he has less than half the teacher's virtue; when one's knowledge surpasses the teacher, only then is he qualified for the transmission.' Many say 'when one's view is equal to the teacher' and 'when the view surpasses the teacher' — this doesn't miss the principle. Wangshan Fazu said, 'There are three kinds of lions: the first transcends sect, with a different eye; the second is shoulder to shoulder, in the same track; the third is shadow and echo, not real.' One who transcends sect with a different eye has a view which goes beyond his teacher, and is capable of being a seedling; one who is shoulder to shoulder in the same track has less than half his teacher's virtue, and is stuck in the present; one who is shadow and echo, not real, is a mixture of fox and jackal, a sheep in a tiger's skin.

"Tiantong brings up how Deshan usually never let even buddhas or patriarchs stand under his cane, but at this

this is sustenance for an adopted son, how can he avoid getting criticism from people of later times?' When Linji left Huangbo, the latter asked him 'Where are you going to go?' Linji said, 'If not south of the river, then north of the river.' Huangbo then hit him; Linji grabbed and held him, and gave him a slap. Huangbo laughed loudly and called to his attendant, 'Bring me my late master Baizhang's meditation brace and desk.' When the attendant brought them, Linji repeatedly shouted, 'Attendant, bring me fire!' Huangbo said, 'Just take them and go — later on you will cut off the tongues of everyone on earth.' Tiantong just knows how to examine the man who transmits the Dharma, but doesn't know that the man who receives the Dharma deserves it even more. At that time if I were Linji, when I heard him say, 'Just take them and go — later on you'll cut off the tongues of everyone on earth,' I'd just say to him, 'If you want to cut off the tongues of everyone on earth, then indeed you should bring fire and burn up today's public case, and just merge with the ordinary.' If I had seen Deshan say, 'So it is, so it is — guard it well on your own,' I would have shouted thunderously and left, and our posterity would not be cut off.

Public Cases from the Empty Valley Collection

BALING'S CHICKENS AND DUCKS

LINQUAN'S INTRODUCTION

A wooden horse neighs in the wind, a clay ox bellows at the moon. In the midst of speechlessness, yet it is possible to be talkative; how should one speak of where it is beyond right and wrong, apart from sameness and difference?

QUOTATION

A monk asked Master Haojian of Baling, "Are the meaning of the patriarchs and the meaning of the teachings the same or different?" He replied, "When chickens are cold they roost in the trees; when ducks are cold they go into the water."

LINQUAN'S COMMENTARY

When chan master Haojian of Xinkai monastery in Baling, Yue province, first came to Yunmen, Yunmen said, "Master Xuefeng said, 'Bodhidharma's come!' I ask you, what about it?" The master said, "Right under your nose." Yunmen said, "The earth spirit rages up, hits Mount Sumeru, leaps up to the brahma heaven, and smashes Indra's nose; why do you hide in Japan?" He said, "Master, don't fool people." Yunmen said, "Right under my nose — what about that?" The master had nothing to say; Yunmen said, "I knew you were a student of words."

After the Master was dwelling in a monastery as a teacher, he didn't write a document of succession; he just presented three pivotal words to Yunmen: a monk asked what the way is, and the master said, "A clear-eyed man falls into a well;" a monk asked what the 'hair-blown sword' is, and the master said, "Each branch of coral supports the moon;" a monk asked what the sect of Kanadeva is, and the master said, "Piling snow in a silver bowl." Yunmen said, "Later on, on the anniversary of my death, you only need to quote these three pivotal words to sufficiently requite my kindness." Subsequently, at memorial services, he actually did thus, as he had been instructed. I say, you should know that the giving of Dharma is inexhaustible; requital of virtue and benevolence extends over past and present.

A monk asked, "Are the meaning of the patriarchs and the meaning of the teachings the same or different?" This monk was very much like picking the moon out of the sky or gold out of sand; in the realm of real purity he created something where there was nothing. After all it was truly said, "Old Xinkai — he's clearly special" — He not only says, "Piling snow in a silver bowl," he also is able to know that chickens and ducks each have their own resting place. What a pity that he causes people to grope without finding where cold and exhausted, dry and deserted. Clearly the patriarchs' meaning and the teachings' meaning are imparted to Touzi, and he sticks them together before the crowd. His verse says,

TOUZI'S VERSE

> *Same or different from the meaning of the*
> * patriarchs — he asks about the origin,*
> *So he uses the fundamental value to give him an*
> * answer.*
> *An imperial command; the night quiet, a man lets*
> * down a hook —*
> *At dawn he takes in the sun together with the*
> * moon.*

Producing understanding from hearing, coloring in the mind; the auspicious grass is rootless, the wise don't esteem it.

As Luopu was standing by Linji, a lecturing monk came to call on Linji; Linji asked, "There is one man who attains understanding from the teachings of the three vehicles, and there is one man who doesn't attain understanding from the teachings of the three vehicles; tell me, are these two men the same or different?" The lecturer said, "If they understand, they're the same; if they don't understand, they're different." Linji looked at Luopu and said, "What about you?" Luopu immediately shouted.

When Yunmen came to Chekiang, prime minister Chen invited him to a meal; as soon as he saw Yunmen, he immediately asked him, "I do not ask about what is in the confucian writings, and the canonical teachings of the three vehicles have their own professors; what is the business of a patchrobed monk's pilgrimage?" Yunmen said, "How many people have you asked?" He said, "I am asking you right now." Yunmen said, "Leaving aside 'right now,' what is the meaning of the teachings?" Chen said, "Yellow scrolls, red rollers." Yunmen said, "These are written words — what is the meaning of the teachings?" Chen said, "When the mouth wants to talk about it, words disappear; when the mind wants to grasp it, thought vanishes." Yunmen said, " 'When the mouth wants to talk about it, words disappear' deals with maintaining verbalization; 'when the mind seeks to grasp it, thought vanishes' deals with false conceptualization — what is the meaning of the teaching?" The prime minister was speechless. Yunmen said, "I've heard that you've read the Lotus scripture — is this true or not?" He said, "It is." Yunmen said, "In the scripture it says, 'All productive labor is not contrary to the character of reality' — tell me, in the heaven beyond perception and nonperception, how many people regress from that state?" The minister was speechless. Yunmen said, "Don't be so careless; even the three greatest scriptures and five classic treatises are given up by monks to specially enter Chan monasteries. Even after ten or twenty years, they still can't do anything — how could you understand, prime minister?" The minister bowed and said, "I am at fault." I say, shame and fear in a bronze face, tolerance on a tin spear.

Now tell me, are the answers of Luopu and Yunmen and the answer of Baling one kind of reimbursement or two kinds? Can you pin it down? Now entering a new market, let the cashier discuss short and long. The old fellow of Baling rowed out into the still waters of the clear source and let down a hook; he didn't mind if the water was cold in the quiet of night — how could he fear the empty boat carrying the moon? If you know that for the chickens and ducks there is no seeking, you naturally won't be in a rush looking up and down for them.

MY PROVINCE IS PEACEFUL

The four eyes are undimmed; the six thieves surrender. Having seen the year of Great Peace in a forest of spears and shields, you find the land of purity in a pile of rubbish. Would you believe it is fundamentally inherent? How could you know it is not sought from another? Stealing leisure in the midst of hurry, how can you understand verbally?

QUOTATION

Yaoshan asked novice Gao, "I hear that Changan is very noisy." The novice said, "My province is peaceful." Yaoshan joyfully said, "Did you realize this from reading scriptures, or from making inquiries?" The novice said, "I didn't get it from reading scriptures or from making inquiries." Yaoshan said, "Many people do not read scriptures or make inquiries—why don't they get it?" The novice said, "I don't say they don't get it—it's just that they don't agree to take it up."

LINQUAN'S COMMENTARY

When novice Gao first called on Yaoshan, Yaoshan asked him, "Where do you come from?" He said, "From Nanyue." Yaoshan asked, "Where are you going?" He said, "To Jiangling to receive the precepts." Yaoshan said, "What is the aim of receiving precepts?" He said, "To escape birth and death." Yaoshan said, "There is someone who doesn't receive the precepts and has no birth and death to escape—do you know?" He said, "Then what is the use of the buddha's precepts?" Yaoshan said, "This novice still has lips and teeth." The novice bowed and withdrew. Daowu came and stood by Yaoshan; Yaoshan said to him, "That limping novice who just came, after all has some life in him." Daowu said, "He's not to be entirely believed yet—you should test him again first." When evening came, Yaoshan went up into the hall; he called, "Where is the novice who came earlier?" Novice Gao came forth from the assembly and stood there; Yaoshan said, "I hear Changan is very noisy; do you know, or not?" The novice said, "My province is peaceful." Fayan said, as an alternative reply, "Who told you?" Yaoshan, seeing that the novice's reply had some basis, again asked, "Did you realize this from reading scriptures, or from making inquiries?" The novice didn't fall into his cage at all; he said, "I didn't get it from reading scriptures or from making inquiries." Yaoshan saw that he couldn't entrap him; using another living road of action, again he said accusingly, "Many people don't read scriptures or make inquiries—why don't they get it?" The novice's whole body was hands and eyes—he wouldn't be tied up or overthrown; he said, "I don't say they don't get it—it's just that they don't agree to take it up." At this point, the cart couldn't be pushed sideways, principle could not be decided crookedly; Yaoshan looked back at Daowu and Yunyan and said, "Didn't you believe what I said?" We might say that to surpass the crowd one must be an outstanding spirit, conquering enemies is a matter for a lion. If you can see through here, only then can you truly say that you are desireless in the midst of desires, unstained while dwelling in the dusts, going through a thicket of a hundred kinds of flowers without a single petal getting on you. If you can forget both clamor and silence, you will surely understand the simultaneous realization of absolute and relative. At this point, how should one judge?

TOUZI'S VERSE

> *Flourishing, perishing; clouds go, clouds come.*
> *He has no country, is utterly free from dust.*
> *On the peak of Mount Sumeru, rootless plants;*
> *Without feeling the spring breeze, the flowers bloom*
>   *of themselves.*

LINQUAN'S COMMENTARY

(Raising a yellow flower,) Worldly affairs—clouds going through a thousand changes; evanescent life—a scene in a dream. Although this is momentarily conveying elation, expressing feelings, there is a deep reason to it. If you are able to act in accordance with what you say, so that mind and mouth are not two, if you can see through here, you will not be fooled by myriad objects—what gain and loss, right and wrong, prosperity and decline, success and defeat can fetter you?

Fengxue said, "If you set up a single atom, the country flourishes and the peasants frown. If you do not set up a single atom, the country perishes and the peasants rest easy." All at once cutting off the setting up and not setting up, what flourishing or perishing can remain? This is all leftovers of inherent emptiness, floating flowers in the eye of the Way. Although coming and going leaves no traces, what about ignorance becoming an obstacle to vision? Just realizing pure spotless clarity, free of even a fine hair, in the echoless mountains you meet a legless stone man, and on top of Mount Sumeru pick rootless auspicious plants. I hope without depending on the spring breeze the fragrance will fill the world; I ask chan followers who have the eye to try to come appreciate it. Do you see? Spiritual sprouts grow where there is land; great enlightenment does not keep a teacher.

Public Cases from the Vacant Hall Collection

JIUFENG, THE ATTENDANT

LINQUAN'S INTRODUCTION

People are tested with words, water is tested with a stick; deep and shallow, high and low—how can they be mixed up? How pitiful—one spot of feelings' dust makes you half light and half dark. If you can lose yourself and follow the others, I dare say then there'd be no regret. Is there not someone who can let go and be free?

QUOTATION

Jiufeng was with Shishuang, serving as his attendant. After Shishuang passed on, the community wanted to ask the senior monk in the hall to succeed him as abbot, but Jiufeng did not agree; he said, "Wait 'till I question him; if he understands the late master's meaning, I will serve him as I did the late master."

So he asked the senior monk, "The late master said, 'Cease, desist, for ten thousand years in an instant, like cold ashes, a dead tree, a censer in an ancient shrine, a strip of white silk'—tell me, what does this illustrate?" The senior monk said, "It illustrates the matter of uniformity." Jiufeng said, "Then you don't understand the late master's meaning yet." The senior monk said, "You don't agree with me? Come set up some incense." Then he lit the incense and said, "If I don't understand the late master's meaning, I couldn't die while this incense smoke is rising." So saying, he sat down and passed away.

Jiufeng then patted him on the back and said, "I don't deny you can die sitting or standing, but when it comes to the late master's meaning, you're not there yet."

LINQUAN'S COMMENTARY

Calling on a teacher, asking about the way, he assisted at the monastery, having personally served as Shishuang's attendant. When Shishuang had died and the community asked the senior monk to succeed as abbot, Jiufeng's examination certainly was reasonable. Thus a scripture says, "Sentient beings are hindered by their understanding; enlightening beings are not yet free from awareness.' How much the more so was this senior monk, who relied on the accomplishment of stillness; if it hadn't been for the attendant not approving him and honestly testing him with adverse and favorable situations, after all revealing seeking, it would be hard to say that the eight winds couldn't move him and that he was always constant and stable for all time.

One day Caoshan saw The Paper-Robed Wayfarer come, and asked him, "Are you not The Paper-Robed Wayfarer?" He said, "I do not presume." Caoshan said, "What is the thing in the paper robe?" He said, "As soon as the skin coat is hung on the body, myriad things are all Thus." Caoshan said, "What is the function in the paper robe?" The wayfarer walked up, said "OK" and died standing. Caoshan said, "You know how to go this way; why don't you come this way?" The wayfarer suddenly opened his eyes and asked, "What about when the real nature of the one life-force does not avail itself of the womb?" Caoshan said, "This is not yet wonderful." He said, "What is wonderful?" Caoshan said, "Using without depending." The Paper-Robed Wayfarer then bade farewell and sat down and passed away. Caoshan then made a verse saying,

> The formless body of complete illumination of the
>   nature of awareness;
> Don't use knowledge and views, misconstruing far
>   and near.
> If thoughts vary, you're blind to the profound
>   essence;
> If the mind differs, you're not close to the path.
> When feelings discriminate myriad things, they
>   submerge the present situation;
> When consciousness perceives many aspects, you
>   lose the original reality.
> If you can clearly understand from such sayings,
> Clearly you're the man of before, without any
>   concern.

This is not different from the attendant Jiufeng not agreeing with the senior monk, particularly since Shishuang's senior monk, though he knew how to go this way, he didn't know how to come this way; The Paper-Robed Wayfarer also knew how to go thus, and also knew how to come thus — still, Caoshan himself did not let him off without making an appearance. On the whole, those whose feelings retain inclination and opposition, and whose viewpoint is onesided and biased, just greedily linger in their tracks, sunk in the void, not caring to 'continue the fragrance, continue the flame.' But tell me, where is the benefit or harm? Here is Danxia, who harmonizes with him; his verse says,

DANXIA'S VERSE

Wearing horns, covered with fur – a different
*   species body.*
Cold ashes, dead tree—dust in the eyes.
Even if he didn't yet understand the late master's
*   meaning,*
Nonetheless his one saying on the verge of going
*   was new.*

LINQUAN'S COMMENTARY

First enlightened, enlightening afterward, self-help and helping others, guiding people to benefit the living— wondrous functions are manifold. In the function which is identical to essence, holding still and letting go rest completely in oneself; in the essence which is identical to function, bringing forth and throwing away depend on no one else. Therefore we wear horns and fur, freely embodying different species, plowing in the clouds under the hazy moon, entering the market place with open hands. Even cold ashes and dead trees, cool, clear and pure, when seen with the true eye, all are defilements. What uniformity can be pinned down?

Although at the time he didn't understand the late master's meaning, Danxia volubly approves of him, saying, "Nonetheless his one saying on the verge of going was new." Although this saying is new, how could it compare to having replied to Jiufeng in the first place when he said, "Then you don't understand the late master's meaning yet." What he said here was no more new or fresh. If so, then what was the necessity of lighting incense and dying while sitting, having someone pat him on the back and say, "You still don't understand the late master's meaning?" Do you know where the freedom to praise or censure, independence in conceding or taking away is? "A patchwork coverlet over my head, myriad concerns cease; at this time this mountain monk understands nothing at all."

LIANGSHAN'S EMPTY AEON

LINQUAN'S INTRODUCTION

A frozen river bursts into flame, an iron tree blooms with flowers—it does not come from the loom of creation; how could it be within the range of yin and yang? Where primordial chaos is not yet differentiated, try to see for sure.

QUOTATION

A monk asked Liangshan, "What is that which is before the empty aeon?" Liangshan said, "The drum which rattles the universe, people of the time don't hear."

LINQUAN'S COMMENTARY

The unbridled wooden horse leaps high before the primordial buddha, the legless stone man walks alone after the emptiness of the aeon; only then will you believe when it's said that inconceivable existence basically is not existent, that real emptiness fundamentally is not empty. Independent, lively standing out, for all time the function is inexhaustible. Thus we know that this thing is not empty, not existent, not one, not two, not the same, not different, not identical, not disparate; try to compare it and you miss, try to discuss it and you're wrong. It is always presented to your face—what a pity that it's cast off behind your head. I deeply pity these folks who try to grasp the moon in the water, not realizing that the moon is in the sky, who try to grasp flowers in the air, not realizing the flowers have no stems. Pursuing an air of fragrance, they mistake the reflection for the head. Searching with all their might, they don't get so much as a bit of hair. That is why Liangshan said, "The drum which rattles the universe, people of the time don't hear." I say, although living beings have ears, how many know the sound? Also see how Danxia settles the harmony; his verse says,

DANXIA'S VERSE

> *Empty space is the drum, Mt. Sumeru is the drum*
> *   stick;*
> *Although those who beat are many, those who hear*
> *   are few.*
> *In the middle of night, a skull awakens from a*
> *   dream;*
> *Though bright moonlight covers his head, he doesn't*
> *   think of returning.*

LINQUAN'S COMMENTARY

Chan master Ji-an of Yanguan in Hangzhou said to his group, "Space is a drum, Mount Sumeru is the drum stick; who knows how to beat it?" No one replied. Nanquan said, "I don't beat this broken drum." I say it's just that you're too lazy. Fayan said as an alternative, "Nanquan doesn't beat it." I say, "I'm just afraid the bystander doesn't know how many beats." Xuedou brought this up and said, "Those who beat are many, those who hear extremely few. I ask, who is the one who knows how to beat it? Don't slander Yanguan. Nanquan said he doesn't beat this broken drum, Fayan said that Nanquan doesn't beat it; both can do nothing, one is even ashamed." He also said, "Nanquan doesn't beat it— does he agree with everyone else or not?" He answered himself, "A thousand year field, eight hundred land-lords." I say, curling the fingers counting from the top, none is real. When you look at it this way, how can we avoid Danxia's saying, "Although those who beat it are many, those who hear it are few." In the middle of the night, the skull first awakens from a dream; in the third watch, the pillar happens to emit light—those with eyes, discern it clearly. Just waiting till you've a head full of moonlight and sideburns of frosty flowers, you collapse in the present and don't think of beyond time. That is why Dongshan said, "On the road, don't go; coming back, turn away from your father." But how can you get it right? Do you know? Without leaving the flower-strewn road you travel throughout the clear sky.

DONGSHAN AND THE GREAT MATTER

LINQUAN'S INTRODUCTION

Looking afar, stop looking nearby; with every thought you should investigate death and life. Discuss the true, not the false; earnestly talk only about the ultimate truth. A clear indication—buy afterwards, try first. Is there anyone who can profitably open shop? Please do.

QUOTATION

Dongshan asked a monk, "In all the world, what thing is most painful?" The monk said, "Hell is most painful."

Dongshan said, "Not so; to wear this robe and not understand the great matter is what is really painful."

The Realized One used the four immeasurable minds of love, compassion, joy, and equanimity to liberate sentient beings; the patriarchs used the three undefiled sciences of morality, concentration, and wisdom to awaken the patch-robed ones. Dongshan points his hand on the summit of the highest mountain; this monk shakes his head at the bottom of the deepest sea. Already this is thanking him for not saying that sugar is most sweet, yellow plum is most bitter. It seems he can hardly forget what is familiar; even seeing the doormen of hell in a dream, he is frightened— he doesn't know that when Devadatta fell into hell for slandering the buddha and Buddha sent Ananda to ask after him and see if he was suffering or not, Devadatta said, "I am in uninterrupted hell, but feel like I'm enjoying the pleasure of the third meditation heaven." Still this monk says hell is most painful. According to the capacity, what a difference, as between sky and earth. That is why Dongshan said, "Not so; to wear this robe and not understand the great matter is what is really painful." This is truly what is called using the heart of a whole lifetime out of pity for a three-year-old child. Although this is holding the ox's head to have it eat grass, still it doesn't exclude adding stripes to a tiger's back. Fortunately we meet Danxia, who in turn exhorts and admonishes;

DANXIA'S VERSE

Boiling cauldrons, furnaces of coals — how many
*   kinds?*
Hell and the three mires are not so painfully bitter.
You should believe the kind words of Xinfeng;
Clothed in monk's vestments, don't be bigheaded.

The ocean of all obstructions from actions all comes from false conceptions. Are boiling cauldrons, furnaces of coals, sword-trees and knife-mountains, hells and the three mires, the only painful things? Because of this Danxia reiterates this meaning in behalf of Donghsan, repeating it in the words of his verse—in ancient and recent times, doting kindness.

In sum, transmigration through the six dispositions, appearing and disappearing in the four forms of birth, all is due to not realizing the treasury of the eye of truth, the ineffable mind of nirvana. When The World-Honored One first attained true enlightenment, he observed that all sentient beings everywhere fully possess the knowledge, wisdom, and virtuous characteristics of The Realized One; just because of their false conceptions and attachments they do not realize it. Is this not what Dongshan is calling the great matter? Therefore Danxia repeats the instruction: "You should believe the kind words of Xinfeng; clothed in monks' vestments, don't be bigheaded." From the end of the Dazhong era of the Tang dynasty, Dongshan received and guided people on Xinfeng Mountain; later he spread the teaching at Dong Mountain (Dongshan) in Gaoan in Yuzhang province. Provisionally opening up the five ranks, he skillfully guided those of higher, middling, and lower faculties, greatly spreading the mystic sound, illuminating the way of the patriarchs. The name Xinfeng comes from the mountain where he stayed.

Now about the words he entrusted; are they kind or not? Should one be bigheaded or not? It is like someone drinking water—what need to ask whether it is cool or warm? Only a clear mind knows of itself.

Sayings of Master Rujing of Tiantong

Rujing lived from 1163 to 1228 and served as abbot and teaching master at several large public monasteries; it was at Tiantong in eastern China that Dogen met Rujing, who was to become the final human teacher and greatest spiritual benefactor of young Dogen. Rujing was descended from the great Cao Dong masters Furung and Danxia; it was he who taught Dogen the 'technique' of 'just sitting', which he used to practice together with the community in the great meditation halls. The following talk about sitting meditation is taken from the *Hokyoki*, Dogen's record of private talks with Rujing; the general talk and the eulogies are from records of Rujing's sayings compiled by other disciples.

Although saints and self-enlightened sages do not become attached to their experience in sitting meditation, they lack great compassion; therefore they are not the same as the buddhas and patriarchs, who considered great compassion foremost and sat in meditation with the vow to save all sentient beings. The outsiders in India also sat in meditation, but they always had three problems; attachment to the experience, false views, and conceit—therefore it is always different from the sitting meditation of the buddhas and patriarchs.

Buddhist disciples also had sitting meditation, but their compassion was weak; they did not penetrate the real character of all things with incisive knowledge—only improving themselves, they cut off the lineage of buddhas; therefore theirs is always different from the sitting meditation of buddhas and patriarchs.

What I mean to say is that buddhas and patriarchs, from their very first inspiration, sit in meditation with the vow to gather together all the qualities of buddhahood; therefore in their sitting meditation they do not forget sentient

91

beings, do not forsake sentient beings — they always have loving thoughts even for insects, and vow to rescue them. Whatever virtures they have, they dedicate to all; therefore the buddhas and patriarchs are always in the world of desire practicing meditation and working on the way. In the world of desire only this world provides the best situation; cultivating all virtues life after life, one attains to gentility and ease of mind.

GENERAL TALK

Kaaa! People, this shout, though before the ancient buddhas, has already missed the point; how much the more so to come here today and shout wildly — what kind of farting this would be. If there is someone who can come forth boldly to smash this shitty mouth, knock out my teeth and stuff them in a shit hole, you can avoid seeing me fooling people with a lot of confusion.

But even this is still raising your fist behind someone's back, raising your voice to stop an echo; yet we set up many gates, to open up a single road — isn't there any one who will come forth?

(A long silence) If there is no one, then I will use a shout for the moment to pile up confusion and fool you people. Kaaa! Here there is host and guest, illumination and function; do you know where it ultimately ends up? If you realize where it ends up, you know where it arises; if you know where it arises, you know where it passes away. If you know where it passes away, you then realize that birth and death both pass away, and ultimate peace appears, in everyday life, appearing in six places. In the eye it is called seeing; you must strip off your eyes till you see nothing at all — then afterwards there is nothing you don't see; only then can it be called seeing.

In the ear it is called hearing; you must block your ears shut till you hear nothing at all — then afterwards there is nothing you don't hear; only then can it be called hearing.

In the nose it is called smelling; you must smash off your nostrils till fragrance and stench are not distinguished — afterwards there is nothing you can't distinguish; only then can it be called smelling.

In the tongue it talks; you must pluck out your tongue, so heaven and earth are wrapped up in silence — afterwards it is effulgent and unbroken; only then can it be called talking.

In the body it is called person; you must slough off the gross elements and not depend on anything — afterwards you manifest form in accordance with kind (of being); only then can it be called person.

In the mind it is called consciousness; you must cut off forever all clinging to objects, so that the three incalculable aeons are empty—afterwards origin and decease do not stop — only this can be called consciousness.

Appearing as above in these six places, without any gap, this is what is meant by there being host and guest, illumination and function, as I said before — host and guest interchange, illumination and function merge. From the buddhas of the past, present, and future and the six generations of ancestral teachers above to the animals of various species, plants, trees, and insects below, all are this one shout — none is left out. Then you see that 'before the appearance of the ancient buddhas' is right now, and right now is 'before the appearance of the ancient buddhas.' They are not two, do not have two separate conditions, because they are not distinct; they are continuous.

According to what I am saying, what is there to shout about or talk about? Basically there is not so much — everyone should get a beating. What mistake is there? What is not mistaken? There are even Linji's four shouts; no harm to move the shoulders while walking — I'll pierce nostrils one by one for you. Bah! 'One shout is like the jewel sword of the diamond king' — a toilet sweeper. 'One shout is like a lion crouching on the ground' — a rat in its nest. 'One shout is like a probing pole, shadowing grass' — a fellow fishing for clams. 'One shout does not function as a shout' — a ghost in front of a skull. Tonight is clear and cool; I call this medicine for a dead horse — even if you can bring this shout to life, how can you avoid the sound of farting?

Even so, tell me, where does it come from, 'before the ancient buddhas appeared?' Can you be sure? If you can get it for sure, then nothing's wrong with wild shouting — you'll avoid seeking it folding your hands at the corner of a rope seat. If you are not yet thus, though, beware of misusing your fists and feet. Bah!

VERSE ON LINJI

> *Making an empty fist,*
> *Threatening the world to death;*
> *Such an ancestral teacher –*
> *An animal, an ass.*

VERSE ON AN ANCIENT SAYING

Yunmen said, "The world is so wide—why put on a seven-strip robe at the sound of a bell?"
   Rujing said,

> *At the sound of the bell I put on a dense web;[1]*
> *The inconceivable function's miraculous powers*
> *Produce a variety of effects.*
> *The thief is a member of the family;*
> *It is necessary to sweep away the tracks –*
> *Only the great peace with no signs*
> *Is really safe and harmonious.*

1. *'Dense web' also alludes to the multitude of appearances of the phenomenal world. This reading is hardly concealed in the phonetic transcription for the Sanskrit word for 'upper robe' – i.e. the 7-strip.*

FUNERAL SPEECHES

SETTING FIRE TO ELDER YI'S BIER

'All things return to one' — living is like wearing your shirt; 'where does the one return?' — dying is like taking off your pants. When life and death are sloughed off and do not concern you at all, the spiritual light of the one path always stands out unique. Ah, the swift flames in the wind flare up — all atoms in all worlds do not interchange.

SETTING FIRE TO A DOCTOR'S BIER

The mortal diseases of humans you can heal, but when you die, who can bring you back to life? I have a simple method, a handful of fire; I will burn for you the medicine gourd. Someone answers, "I'm alive, revived" — tell me, how do you prove it? (describing a circle with the fire-brand) Ah, the original face has no birth or death; spring is in the plum flowers, entering a painted picture.

Life of Zen Master Dogen of Eihei

from *Biographical Extracts of the Original Stream,* compiled by zen master Geppa

The zen master's name was Dogen. He was from Kyoto. His lay surname was Minamoto, and he was a descendant of emperor Murakami (r. 946-967). He left society as a youth and was ordained by Koen of Yokogawa. Before many years had passed, he had read the whole buddhist canon two times.

One day he resolved upon that which is outside the teachings (zen); he left and called on Eisai of Kennin monastery and Gyoyu at Jomyo monastery. Eventually he attained the Dharma in the tenth generation of the Huanglong succession.[1]

When he heard someone extolling the zen way in Sung China, he went right to China on a merchant ship. He went to ask about the quick way to enter the path from Liaopa Wuji at Tiantong mountain, Cheying Ruyan at Jin Shan, Yuankao at Wannian monastery, Sitiao at Xiaosuian: he didn't agree with any of them — he thought to himself that there was no teacher in China better than he himself.

When he first lay down his staff at Tiantong, the community decided to place him as a novice[2] because he was from another country. The master was not happy about this, and appealed in writing to the emperor; after three times he finally got his wish. From this his name was heard far and wide.

The next year he met Rujing, who had come to dwell at Tiantong. The master greeted him joyfully, and as soon as Rujing saw him, he esteemed him as a vessel of Dharma. The master submitted to him in all sincerity and entered his room.[3] He meditated diligently day and night, never lying down.

One night as Rujing was passing through the hall, he saw a monk sitting dozing and said, "For this affair it is necessary to shed body and mind — if you just sleep like this, when will you ever have today's affair?" Then he took off his slipper and hit the monk. The master, nearby, got the message and was greatly enlightened. The next day he went to the abbot's quarters; Rujing laughed and said, "The shedding is shed." At that time Kuangping of Fuzhou was standing by as Rujing's attendant; he said, "It is not a small thing, that a foreigner has attained such a great matter." The master bowed. After this he worked most earnestly and attained all the secrets.

When he was taking his leave to return east, Rujing imparted to him the essential teachings of the Dong succession[4] and the patched robe of master Furong, saying, "You should go back east forthwith; just spread the teaching so it will never end." The master accepted with bowed head and finally returned. When he began to teach in Fukakusa, south of Kyoto, everywhere they honored him as the first patriarch of Soto zen in Japan.

The master said, "I did not visit many monasteries, but I happened to meet my late teacher at Tiantong and directly realized that my eyes are horizontal and my nose is vertical; I was not to be fooled by anyone. Then I returned home with empty hands. Thus I have no Buddhism at all; I just pass the time as it goes: every morning the sun rises in the east, every night the moon sets in the west. When the clouds recede the mountain rises appear; when the rain has passed, the surrounding hills are low. Ultimately, how is it? Every four years is leap year, the cock crows at dawn."

Later in life he built Eihei, Sanctuary of Eternal Peace, in Echizen province, and lived there. Before long people came in droves. His monastery regulations were just like those of Tiantong: it was the first strictly zen monastery in Japan. At that time (1243-47) the emperor (Go-Fukakusa) sent down an edict granting him a purple vestment of honor and the title Zen Master of Buddhism. A chamberlain brought the order; after giving thanks for the favor, he strongly refused it several times, but the emperor would not allow this. So Dogen eventually took it and offered a poem which said,

> *Though the mountain of Eihei is insignificant*
> *The imperial order is repeated in earnest:*
> *After all I am laughed at by monkeys and cranes,*
> *An old man in a purple robe.*

The emperor long admired him.

The master was fond of seclusion and built a separate hut

under Crystal Cliff as a retirement retreat. He wrote poems
such as

> The ancestral way which came from the west, I
>   have brought east—
> Fishing in the moonlight, pillowing in the clouds, I
>   have tried to emulate the ancient way.
> The flying red dust of the conventional world cannot
>   reach
> This reed hut on a snowy night deep in the
>   mountains.

and

> The wind is cold in my three room reed house:
> Observing my nose [5] I first come upon the fragrance
>   of autumn chrysanthemums.
> Even with an iron or a bronze eye, who could
>   discern?
> In Eihei nine times I have seen the fall.

The assistant commander of the Taira, Tokiyori, esteemed the master's way and several times called him to
stay at famous temples, but he didn't go. After a long time
the master went on his own to call on him. The assistant
commander greeted him and saw him off; he paid obeisance to Dogen as a disciple, and asked him about the
path and received the precepts from him. The master
passed the year and then returned.

In the end he summoned his disciple Ejo and imparted
his final instructions. He then wrote a verse and died. The
verse said,

> Fifty four years illuminating the highest heaven,
> I leap into the universe.
> Ah, there is no place to look for my whole body:
> I fall living into hades.

He was fifty four, and had been a monk for thirty-seven
years. His monument was built at Eihei, and he was entitled Joyo, Heir to the Sun.

NOTES TO BIOGRAPHY OF DOGEN

1. Huanglong was one of the branches of the Linji (Rinzai) school of zen in China, to which Eisai had succeeded. Dogen also studied with Myozen at Kennin monastery; Myozen was considered Eisai's foremost disciple.

2. In a monks' hall or meditation hall, the seating arrangement is determined by seniority or ordination age.

3. Entering a zen master's room for personal encounter and instruction is a special part of zen practice; Rujing is said to have allowed Dogen to enter his room without formality, to discuss anything he wanted; the *Hokyoki* mentioned previously was a record of Dogen's conversations with Rujing in his room.

4. This probably refers to the teaching of the five ranks of Dong Shan, the *Baojing sanmei* and *Can Tong Qui:* secret oral instruction on the application and interpretation of these formulae seems to have been part of the 'transmission of Dharma' from a teacher to an awakened disciple.

5. Fixing the attention on the nose is one method of breath contemplation; it is also called 'stopping.'

Informal Talks

From the *Record of Sayings of Zen Master Dogen of Eihei*

AT THE BEGINNING OF SUMMER RETREAT

Once when Zikong was at Tiantong monastery in Siming, at the beginning of a summer retreat he said, "For people in meditation the most important thing is that the nostrils[1] be right; then the eyes must be thoroughly clear. Then it's important to realize the source and understand the explanation, and after that capability and its actualization are equally realized — only then can you enter among enlightened ones and demons as well, where oneself and others succeed together at once." What does it mean?

When the nostrils are right, everything is right. It is like a man in a house; if the master is upright, his family is naturally influenced. But how can you get your nostrils straight? An ancient sage said. "Certainty does not drift into a second thought; only therein you can enter the gate to our school." Did he not set an example for you that was before the birth of your parents?

Although the man of old said that certainty does not drift into second thoughts, I dare ask you people, what is the first thought? Tonight at Eihei I do not spare the effort to speak: I tell you, the ninety day period starts tomorrow; don't go beyond the rules — sitting on a cushion, with no other concerns, celebrating the great peace in empty silence all day long.

AT THE END OF SUMMER RETREAT

Describing a circle in the air, he said,

This is an immeasurably great matter: all the enlightened

ones of past, present and future comprehend this, the successive generations of ancestral teachers realized this, people searching out the way investigate this. If you can get it in your daily activities, you will actually go a step beyond the enlightened ancestors. Have you read how Zhao Zhou asked Daci, "What is the substance of wisdom?" Daci said, "What is the substance of wisdom?" Zhao Zhou laughed aloud. The next day as Zhao Zhou was sweeping the ground, Daci said, "What is the substance of wisdom?" Zhao Zhou threw down the broom and laughed loudly. People, the meeting of two ancient buddhas, Zhao Zhou and Daci, is after all strange and remote; today we are about to dissolve the retreat — how will you assess it? Yesterday a feast, today a bowl of gruel. But say, were those ancients the same, or different? (a long pause) If Daci had asked again, it would renew Zhao Zhou's laughter again. You have been standing for a long time, compassionate ones; please take care.

ON A WINTER NIGHT

When the great achievement is perfected, born in one day, myriad things return to the source — then you see what is precious. That is why it is said, "All the worlds are one of your eyes — all worlds are yourself, all worlds are your aura; all worlds are a gate of liberation. Where do you not realize enlightenment? Where do you not explain what is what and guide people?" And haven't you heard it said that the Guardian of Enlightenment[2] didn't come down from the heaven of satisfaction — the single sphere is everywhere.[3]

ON THE WINTER SOLSTICE

The informal talk is a tradition of the buddhas and enlightened ancestors. We have never heard of it being practiced in Japan in former times — we at Eihei have transmitted this for the first time, doing it for twenty years now.

The ancestral teacher Bodhidharma came from the west and the true teaching entered China; and the ancestral teachers of former ages called this the family custom — not to practice what the buddhas and ancestors did not practice, not to wear anything that is not the robe of righteousness of the buddhas and ancestors, to give up fame and profit, abandon the sense of others and self, to live, secluded in mountains and valleys, never leaving meditation communes, to treasure a little bit of time as most valuable, not worrying about things, but concentrate wholly on understanding the way — this is the tradition of the buddhas and ancestors, the eye of humans and gods. But to be a good teacher it is necessary to practice for immeasurable aeons. People, do you want to see an immeasurable aeon? (he snapped his fingers) Just this is it. Can you say it is inherent? Can you say it is cultivated? If you can see here, this is time passing, years changing, when winter ends spring returns — occupying the ten directions, mystically penetrating past present and future, the old year actually doesn't go, the new year actually doesn't come. Coming and going don't mix — new and old are unrelated. Thus a monk asked Shimen "How is it when the year is ended?" Shimen said, "In the east village old Wong burns paper money offerings in the night." A monk asked Kaixian how it is when the year is ended; Kaixian said, "As of old, early spring is still cold." Tonight if a monk asked me how it is at the end of the year, I would just say to him that in the village up ahead in the deep snow last night a twig sprouted. It's cold and you've been standing a long time.

NOTES TO INFORMAL TALKS

1. The nostrils, the passage of breath, are very important in the physical aspect of meditation; the tuning of the mind to the breath, with the breath, is a basic 'exercise' — its importance is noted in Keizan's *Zazen Yojinki*, a translation of which appears

later in this volume. Metaphorically, the nostrils represent the lifeline, which for buddhists is the *bodhicitta*, the heart, the spirit of enlightenment, the will to undertake acts only for the sake of the enlightenment and liberation of all beings.

2. The Guardian of Enlightenment is a translation of the name given to Shakyamuni when he was still a bodhisattva in Tusita, the heaven of satisfaction, or happiness, where great spiritual heroes live before appearing in this world as buddhas.

3. The word rendered as sphere means also *mandala:* myriad scenes in one scene, ultimately with no coming or going.

Talks from the *Shobogenzozuimonki*

'Record of things heard from the Treasury of the Eye of the True Teaching' made by Ejo based on Dogen's talks

Student's first task should be to abandon your idea of your self. To abandon your idea of your self means that you should not be attached to this body.[1] Even if you have understood the sayings of the ancients and sit all the time like iron or stone, if you remain attached to this body, it is impossible to attain the way of the buddhas and enlightened ancestors, even in myriad aeons over a thousand lifetimes. It should be needless to say that even if you have understood the provisional and true doctrines and the right teaching of the esoteric and exoteric meanings, if you have not given up the feeling of attachment to your bodily self, you are uselessly counting others' treasures without a halfpenny of your own.

I only ask that students sit quiet and examine the beginning and end of this body in a rational manner.

Body, limbs, hair and flesh come from the cells of father and mother — once the breath stops they are strewn in the mountains and fields, eventually turning into mud; what can you hold onto as your bodily self? We can see this all the more from the point of view of elements; in the clustering and disintegration of eighteen elements,[2] what can you define as your body? Although inside the teachings and outside the teachings[3] differ, they are the same in considering the ungraspability of one's own body, its beginning or end, as a point to be aware of in the practice of the way. If you realize this principle, the true way of enlightenment is something obviously so.

If those who study the way do not attain enlightenment, it is because they keep their old views. Though nobody knows who taught them originally, they think that the mind is thought and discernment; if you tell them that the mind is grass and trees, they won't believe you. They think a buddha must have physical signs of greatness and distinction, with an aura of light; they are startled when it is said that buddha is tiles and pebbles. This attachment to views is not inherited from the father or taught by the mother; these ideas are just things you have come to believe for no reason just because you have been hearing people say so for so long.

Therefore, now, since it is the definitive teaching of the buddhas and ancestors, if they say that mind is grasses and trees, realize that grasses and trees are mind; if they say buddha is tile and pebbles, believe that tiles and pebbles are buddha; go on thus giving up your original convictions and attachments, you can attain the way.

An ancient said, "Though sun and moon are bright, floating clouds cover them; though clusters of flowers bloom, the autumn wind destroys them." This is quoted in the *Dengguan zhiyao*, 'essentials of the Dengguan government', as a metaphor for a wise king and evil ministers. Now I say that though the clouds may cover, they won't last long; though the autumn wind ravages, they will bloom again. Even though the ministers be evil, if the wisdom and goodness of the king is more powerful, he won't be influenced. Now to concentrate on the way of enlightenment should also be like this; no matter how bad a state of mind you may get into, if you hold out over the long run, the floating clouds will disappear and the autumn wind will cease. That is a fact.

The actions of people of the path have some meaning to them, whether they are good or bad actions; they cannot be judged by ordinary standards. In ancient times the high priest Eshin one day had someone drive away a deer he had seen eating grass in the garden one day. Someone asked, "The master seems to have no compassion; would you hurt this animal by begrudging it some grass?" The high priest said, "It's not like that. If I didn't chase it away, this deer might eventually become used to humans and get killed when he runs into a vicious man."

So you can see that though it seemed cruel to drive away the deer, the fact was that came from his deep compassion.

NOTES

1.   The word for 'body' also connotes social status and wealth, as well as 'self'.

2.   The eighteen elements are the six senses, their fields, and their consciousnesses; these are considered to be relative reality in the consciousness-only schools of buddhism; on this relative reality is posited a fictional one, obscuring the real reality — relativity, or absence of selfness in anything — contained in the relative reality.

3.   In the traditional chan-zen custom, schools based on scriptures are called teaching or doctrinal schools, in contrast to zen, the scriptureless school; however, there is a profounder sense of the distinction, in that what is outside the teachings refers to right now — what the ancients called the matter of today, progressive enlightenment, transcending the buddhas.

BIOGRAPHIES OF JAPANESE ZEN MASTERS

Ejo of Eihei

The master's initiatory name was Ejo; he was styled Koun (Solitary Cloud). He was from Kyoto; his lay surname was Fujiwara and he was a descendant of the prime minister Tamekichi of the Kujo branch of that clan.

Ever since childhood he did not like to live in society; he first took Enno of Yokogawa as his teacher, shaved his head, put on monks' clothes, and was fully ordained. He studied the essentials of the scholastic schools, and gained a reputation. One day he lamented, "The four schools of Kusha (Abhidharmakosa), Jojitsu (Satyasiddhi), Sanron (Madhyamika), and Hosso (Vijnanavada and Dharmalaksana) are all studies of the compounded; the two doors of cessation and insight (Tendai) and pure land (buddha name remembrance) still do not exhaust the profound mystery."

Then he knew these were not the boat for leaving the world; so he gave them up and called on Kakuen at Tomine and asked about the teaching of seeing reality to realize buddhahood.[1] Kakuen esteemed him deeply as a vessel of Dharma.

Next he called on zen master Dogen at Kennin monastery. Dogen cited the saying "one hair pierces myriad holes" to question him closely. The master silently believed in Dogen and submitted to him. After that he had no desire to go anywhere else, so he changed his robe and stayed there.

Before long Dogen moved to Fukakusa and the master went along with him. He observed and investigated day in and day out, never careless in his actions. One day in the hall, just as he was setting out his bowl, he suddenly attained enlightenment. He immediately went with full ceremony into Dogen's room.[2] Dogen asked him, "What have you understood?" Ejo said, "I do not ask about the one hair; what are the myriad holes?" Dogen laughed and said, "Pierced." Ejo bowed. Afterwards he asked to serve as Dogen's personal attendant, taking care of his robes and bowl. For twenty years he never left his seat beside Dogen, except for a dozen or so days when he was sick.

One day Dogen said to the master, "I first had you take care of monastery work because I wanted to make the teaching last. Although you are older than me, you will be able to spread my school for many years. Work on this." At this point the master Ejo began to expound the teaching too; as Dogen heard him speak, he explained the subtleties for him.

When Dogen died, the master Ejo succeeded him and led the congregation, with no sign of laziness or weariness day or night, in cold or heat. He took the bearing of the teaching of the school as his own responsibility, and the whole congregation, which never numbered less than fifty, gladly obeyed him. Great ministers and important officials came to him and paid obeisance. Henceforth the To succession[3] would flourish greatly.

Late in life he entrusted the teaching to Tettsu. Having personally transmitted his bequest and final teachings, he wrote a verse and died sitting.

The master Ejo was always strong and sturdy by nature, capable of austere practice. He used to lead followers out to Nakahama in the district to practice austerities and carry on the teaching.

1. This refers to the Bodhidharma sect, started in Japan by Kakuen's teacher Dainichi Nonin, a Tendai monk who specialized in meditation according to the zen tradition transmitted by Saicho in the early ninth century.

2. Full ceremony means at least three bows before and after and proper manner of speech and physical deportment.

3. Geppa's collection of biographies refers to what we call Soto zen to the To succession, referring to Tozan (Dong Shan), the ancestor; Dogen's lineage was through Yunju (Ungo), not Cao Shan (Sozan), and Japanese tradition has it that the Cao (So) of Cao Dong (SoTo) comes from Caoqi (Sokei), a place name referring to the illustrious sixth patriarch of Chan, Huineng (Eno).

Gikai of Daijo

The zen master's initiatory name was Gikai; he was styled Tettsu. He was from Etchu, and his lay surname was Fujiwara. He was a distant descendant of the general Toshihito. When he was young he served Ekan at Hachaku temple as his teacher, and studied the three scriptures of the pure land teaching, the Surangama Scripture,[1] the teaching (of zen) of seeing reality, and others. After he was fully ordained he left and travelled around; first he called on Zen master Dogen at Fukakusa. He was strong and pure by nature — he worked at chores and practiced meditation every day, excelling all others. When he heard Dogen say in a lecture, "This truth abides in the state of objective reality; the features of the world are permanent[2] — in the spring scenery the hundred flowers are red;

doves are crying in the willows," he suddenly had an insight.

Before long he moved to Eihei with Dogen; the master asked to be water steward, and personally carried water from Hakkyoku peak. He worked for the community for years. Because he was capable of hard work, Dogen appointed him chief cook and monastery supervisor at the same time. So day and night he took care of a hundred matters, without tiring; in between he worked on meditation even more than others in the community. Dogen called him a true worker on the way.

Later, when Ejo inherited the seat at Eihei, the master Gikai assisted him. One day when he went to the abbot's room, Ejo asked, "How do you understand the shedding of body and mind?" Gikai said, "'I knew barbarians had red beards; here is another red bearded barbarian.'"[3] Ejo agreed with him. Subsequently Ejo used differentiating stories[4] of past and present to refine him thoroughly. After a long time at this he obtained the teaching.[5]

He aspired to cause the school to flourish, and eventually crossed the great waves to far off China. He travelled around there, observing the style of zen both east and west of the Che river,[6] seeing their halls and rooms and what was in them; he drew pictures of everything and came back. Ejo greeted him joyfully and abdicated his seat as abbot of the monastery to him. The master Gikai opened the hall and expounded the teaching, causing the school of Eihei to prosper greatly.

Later in life he changed Daijo teaching temple in Kaga into a zen monastery and dwelt there. The master was respectful and solemn in dealing with the community; his teaching style was most lofty, and everywhere they looked up to him, calling him the reviver of the To succession.

At the end he beat the drum and announced to the community that he had entrusted the teaching to Jokin. He also explained the process of conceiving the determination

for enlightenment and travel for study. Finally he wrote a
verse:

> *Seven upsets, eight downfalls, ninety-one years —*
> *Reed flowers covered with snow,*
> *Day and night the moon is full.*

NOTES

1. This scripture has long been popular in Chinese chan circles,
but Dogen did not approve of it.

2. This is a saying taken from the *Saddharmapundarikasutra,* the
Lotus scripture, the section on methods of guidance.

3. This is from the sayings of Baizhang; it also appears in
Wumenguan (Mumonkan) 2.

4. These are stories involving a shift, a point of transformation,
activation, discriminating knowledge; these are given to students
after they have passed through sayings such as "No," or just sitting with no thought or understanding.

5. This can mean he fully realized the import and application of
the teaching, but it also seems to have come to mean the personal
encounter in which not only are the perspective of teacher and
disciple merged, but an explicit design or illustration is articu-
lated, even using sometimes cryptic ancient zen writings as a
basis, as a seal of the transmission of the oral tradition of the
lineage.

6. This is the central coastal area of eastern China, containing
large urban centers of the Sung dynasty, and large public monasteries.

Jokin of Eiko

The zen master's initiatory name was Jokin; he was styled
Keizan. He was entitled Zen Master with Enlightened

Compassion; this was a posthumous title granted by the emperor of the southern court. He was from Etchu, and his lay surname was Kubara.

When he was a child he took master Ejo as his teacher and shaved his head and put on monk's clothing. When zen master Gikai succeeded to the seat to lead the community at Eihei, the master Jokin served as Gikai's personal attendant, taking care of his robes and bowl. One time when he entered Gikai's room, Gikai asked him, "Can you bring forth the ordinary mind?" As Jokin tried to say something, Gikai hit him right on the mouth; Jokin was at a loss, and at this point his feeling of doubt blazed. One night as he was in the hall sitting in concentration, he suddenly heard the wind at the window and had a powerful insight. Gikai deeply approved of him. After a long time Gikai entrusted the teaching to Jokin, who finally succeeded to the seat at Daijo, having had for years the complete ability, transcending the teacher.

When he reopened the Eiko monastery of eternal light and lived there, lords and officials came to him when they heard of him; his influence was greatest in his time. One day he said to his student Meiho, "On the spiritual mountain there was a leader of the assembly (Mahakasyapa) who shared the teaching seat (with Shakyamuni Buddha); at Caoqi there were leaders of the assembly who shared the teaching. Here at Eiko today I too am making an assembly leader to take part in teaching." Then with a verse he bestowed the robe — "The flaming man under the lamp of eternal light — shining through the aeon's sky, the atmosphere is new. The jutting Peak of Brilliance* is hard to conceal; his whole capability turns over, revealing the whole body."

Thereafter the master Jokin never drummed his lips (spoke much) to the assembly; late in life he changed the disciplinary monastery Soji into a zen place and stayed

---

* This refers to Meiho.

there. After a long time at it, he had had enough of temple business, so he gave the abbacy to Gazan, extending a collateral branch of the teaching. The master Jokin always liked to travel, so when he had retired from his duties he wandered around with a broken rainhat and a skinny cane, meeting people wherever he went, and crowds of people submitted to him.

KEIZAN JOKIN'S *ZAZEN YOJINKI*

What to be aware of in zazen, sitting meditation

Zazen just lets people illumine the mind and rest easy in their fundamental endowment. This is called showing the original face and revealing the scenery of the basic ground. Mind and body drop off, detached whether sitting or lying down. Therefore we do not think of good or bad, and can transcend the ordinary and the holy, pass beyond all conception of illusion and enlightenment, leave the bounds of sentient beings and buddhas entirely.

So, putting a stop to all concerns, casting off all attachments, not doing anything at all, the six senses inactive — who is this, whose name has never been known, cannot be considered body, cannot be considered mind? When you try to think of it, thought vanishes; when you try to speak of it, words come to an end. Like an idiot, like an ignoramus, high as a mountain, deep as an ocean, not showing the peak or the invisible depths — shining without thinking, the source is clear in silent explanation.

Occupying sky and earth, one's whole body alone is manifest; a person of immeasurable greatness — like one who has died utterly, whose eyes are not clouded by anything, whose feet are not supported by anything — where is there any dust? What is a barrier? The clear water never had front or back, space will never have inside or out. Crystal clear and naturally radiant before form and void are separated, how can object and knowledge exist?

This has always been with us, but it has never had a name. The third patriarch, a great teacher, temporarily called it mind; the venerable Nagarjuna provisionally called it body[1] — seeing the essence and form of the enlightened, manifesting the bodies of all buddhas, this, symbolized by the full moon, has neither lack nor excess. It is this mind which is enlightened itself; the light of one's own mind flashes through the past and shines through the present. Mastering Nagarjuna's magic symbol, achieving the concentration of all buddhas, the mind has no sign of duality, while bodies yet differ in appearance. Only mind, only body — their difference and sameness are not the issue; mind changes into body, and when the body appears they are distinguished. As soon as one wave moves, ten thousand waves come following; the moment mental discrimination arises, myriad things burst forth. That is to say that the four main elements and five clusters eventually combine, the four limbs and five senses suddenly appear, and so on down to the thirty six parts of the body, the twelve fold causal nexus; fabrication flows along, developing continuity — it only exists because of the combining of many elements.

Therefore the mind is like the ocean water, the body is like the waves. As there are no waves without water and no water without waves, water and waves are not separate, motion and stillness are not different. Therefore it is said, "The real person coming and going living and dying — the imperishable body of the four elements and five clusters."[2]

Now zazen is going right into the ocean of enlightenment, thus manifesting the body of all buddhas. The innate inconceivably clear mind is suddenly revealed and the original light finally shines everywhere. There is no increase or decrease in the ocean, and the waves never turn back. Therefore the enlightened ones have appeared in the world for the one great purpose of having people realize the knowledge and vision of enlightenment. And they had a peaceful, impeccable subtle art, called zazen, which is the state of absorption that is king of all states of concentration. If you once rest in this absorption, then you directly illumine the mind — so we realize it is the main gate to the way of enlightenment.

Those who wish to illumine the mind should give up various mixed-up knowledge and interpretation, cast away both conventional and buddhist principles, cut off all delusive sentiments, and manifest the one truly real mind — the clouds of illusion clear up, the mind moon shines anew. The Buddha said, "Learning and thinking are like being outside the door; sitting in meditation is returning home to sit in peace." How true this is! While learning and thinking, views have not stopped and the mind is still stuck — that is why it is like being outside the door. But in this sitting meditation, zazen, everything is at rest and you penetrate everywhere — thus it is like returning home to sit in peace.

The afflictions of the five obscurations[3] all come from ignorance, and ignorance means not understanding yourself. Zazen is understanding yourself. Even though you have eliminated the five obscurations, if you have not eliminated ignorance, you are not a buddha or an ancestor. If you want to eliminate ignorance, zazen to discern the path is the most essential secret.

An ancient said, "When confusion ceases, tranquility comes; when tranquility comes, wisdom appears, and when wisdom appears reality is seen." If you want to put an end to your illusion you must stop thinking of good and bad and must give up all involvement in activity; the mind not thinking and the body not doing is the most essential point. When delusive attachments end, illusion dies out. When illusion dies out, the unchanging essence is revealed and you are always clearly aware of it. It is not absolute quiescence, it is not activity.

Hence you should avoid all arts and crafts, medical prescription and augury, as well as songs and dance and music, disputation, meaningless talk, and honor and profit. Though poetry and song can be an aid to clarifying the mind, still you should not be fond of making them; to give up writing and calligraphy is the superior precedent of the people of the way, the best way for harmonizing the mind.

You should not be attached to either fine clothing or dirty rags. Fine clothing instigates greed, and there is also the fear of theft — therefore it is a hindrance to someone on the way. To refuse it when someone gives it for some reason is a praiseworthy act exemplified from ancient times. Even if you happen to have fine clothing, still don't be concerned about taking care of it; if thieves take it, don't chase after it or regret the loss. Old dirty clothes, washed, mended, and completely cleaned, should be worn; if you don't get rid of the dirt you'll get cold and become sick — this too causes obstruction on the way. Although we are not to be anxious for our lives, if clothing, food, and sleep are not sufficient, this is called the three insufficiencies, and are all causes of regression.

Any living things, hard things, and spoiled things — impure food — should not be eaten; with gurgling and churning in the belly, heat and discomfort of body and mind, there will be difficulty in sitting. Do not indulge in attachment to fine food — not only will your body and mind be uncomfortable, but it means you are still greedy. You should take enough food just to support life; don't savor its taste. If you sit after having eaten your fill it can cause illness. After big or small meals, don't sit right away; rather, wait a while before sitting. In general, mendicant monks should be moderate in eating; that means to limit their portions, eat two parts of three and leave one part. All usual medicaments, sesame, wild yams, etc., can be eaten. This is the essential technique of tuning the body.

When sitting in zazen, do not lean against any wall, meditation brace or screen. Also don't sit in a windy place or up on a high exposed place. These are causes of illness. When sitting in meditation, your body may seem hot or cold, uneasy or comfortable, sometimes stiff, sometimes loose, sometimes heavy, sometimes light, sometimes startled awake. This is all because the breath is not in tune and needs to be tuned. The way of tuning the breath is as follows: open your mouth, letting the breath be, long or short, gradually harmonizing it; following it for a while, when a sense of awareness comes, the breath is then in good tune. After that let the breath pass naturally through the nose.

The mind may seem to sink away or float off, sometimes it seems dull, sometimes it seems sharp. Sometimes you see through outside the room, sometimes you can see through your body, sometimes you see forms of buddhas or bodhisattvas. Sometimes you comprehend scriptures or treatises. Extraordinary things like this are diseases from lack of harmony between awareness and breath. When they happen, sit with the mind resting in the lap. If the mind sinks into torpor, rest your mind between your eyes on your hairline (three inches above the center of the eyebrows). If your mind is distracted and scattered, rest your mind on the tip of your nose and your lower belly (one and a half inches below the navel). When sitting all the time rest the mind in the left palm. When you sit for a long time, though you do not force the mind to be calm, it will naturally not be scattered.

Now as for the ancient teachings, though they are traditional lessons for illuminating the mind, don't read, write, or listen to them too much — too much causes disturbance to the mind. In general, anything that wears out body and mind can cause illness. Don't sit where there are fires, floods, or bandits, or by the sea, near wineshops, brothels, or where widows, virgins, or singing girls are. Don't hang around kings, important officials, powerful people, or people full of lust and eager for name and fame, or tellers of tales. As for mass buddhist services and large construction projects, though they are good things, people who are concentrating only on sitting should not do them.

Don't be fond of preaching and teaching, for distraction and scattered thoughts come from this. Don't take delight in crowds or seek for disciples. Don't study or practice too many things. Don't sit where it is extremely bright or dark, extremely cold or hot, or around roustabouts and playgirls. You can stay in a monastery where there is a real teacher, deep in the mountains and hidden valleys. Green waters and verdant mountains are the place to walk in meditation; by the streams, under the trees are places to clear the mind. Observe impermanence, never forget it; this urges on the will to seek enlightenment.

A sitting mat should be spread thick for comfortable sitting, and the place of practice should be clean — always burn incense and offer flowers: the good spirits who guard the true teaching, as well as buddhas and bodhisattvas, will cast their shadows there and give protection. If you place an image of a buddha, bodhisattva, or saint there, no evil demon or spirit can get at you.

Always abide in great compassion, and dedicate the boundless power of sitting meditation to all living beings. Don't become proud, conceited or self-righteous — these are qualities of outsiders and ordinary people. Remember the vow to end afflictions, the vow to realize enlightenment. Just sitting, not doing anything at all, is the essential technique for penetrating zen. Always wash your eyes and feet (before zazen). With body and mind at ease, be-

117

haviour harmonious, abandon worldly feelings and don't cling to feelings of the way.

Although one should not begrudge the teaching, don't speak about it unless you are asked — then hold your peace for three requests, comply if there is a fourth request in earnest. Of ten things you would say, leave off nine. Mold growing around the mouth, like a fan in winter, like a bell hung in the air, not questioning the wind from all directions — this is characteristic of people of the way. Just go by the principle of the teaching[4], don't care about the person; go by the path and do not congratulate yourself — this is the most important point to remember.

Zazen is not concerned with teaching, practice, or realization, yet it contains these three aspects. That is to say, the criterion of realization depends on enlightenment — this is not the spirit of zazen. Practice is based on genuine application — this is not the spirit of zazen. Teaching is based on eliminating evil and cultivating goodness — this is not the spirit of zazen. Although teaching is established within zen, it is not ordinary teaching; it is direct pointing, simply communicating the way, speaking with the whole body. The words have no sentences or phrases; where ideas are ended the reason exhausted, one word comprehends the ten directions. And yet not a single hair is raised — is this not the true teaching of the buddhas and enlightened ancestors?

And although we speak of practice, it is practice without any doing. That is to say, the body doesn't do anything, the mouth does not recite anything,[5] the mind does not think anything over, the six senses are naturally pure and clear, not affected by anything. This is not the sixteen-fold practice of the buddhist disciples[6] or the twelve-fold practice of those enlightened through understanding of causality,[7] or the six ways of transcendental practice undertaking myriad actions done by bodhisattvas;[8] not doing anything at all, it is therefore called buddhahood, the state of enlightenment.

Just resting in the absorption self-experienced by all enlightened ones, roaming at play in the four peaceful and blissful practices of bodhisattvas,[9] is this not the profound, inconceivable practice of buddhas and ancestors?

Though we may speak of realization, this is realization without realization, this is the absorption in the king of concentration, the state of awareness in which you discover knowledge of birthlessness, all knowledge, and spontaneous knowledge;[10] it is the gate of illumination through which the wisdom of the realized ones[11] opens up, produced by the method of practice of great ease. It transcends the patterns of holy and ordinary, goes beyond the sense of confusion and understanding; is this not the realization of innate great enlightment?

Also zazen is not concerned with discipline, concentration, or wisdom, but contains these three studies. That is, discipline is to prevent wrong and stop evil; in zazen we see the whole substance as non dual, cast aside myriad concerns and lay to rest all entanglements. Not concerned with the buddhist way or the worldly way, forgetting feelings about the path as well as mundane feelings, no affirmation or denial, no good or bad — what is there to prevent or stop? This is the formless discipline of the mind ground.

Concentration means undivided contemplation; in zazen we slough off body and mind, abandon confusion and understanding, immutable and imperturbable, not acting, not befuddled, like an idiot, like a dunce, like a mountain, like an ocean, no trace of either motion or stillness arises — concentrated without any sign of concentration, because there is no form of concentration, it is called great concentration.

Wisdom is discerning comprehension; in zazen knowledge disappears of itself, mind and discriminating con-

sciousness is forever forgotten. The wisdom eye throughout the body has no discernment, but clearly sees the essence of buddhahood; fundamentally unconfused, cutting
off the conceptual faculty, open and clearly shining all the
way through, this is wisdom without any sign of wisdom;
because it has no sign of wisdom it is called great wisdom.

The teachings expounded by the buddhas in their lifetimes are all contained in discipline (morality), concentration (meditation), and wisdom (knowledge); in this zazen,
there is no discipline that is not maintained, no concentration that is not cultivated, no wisdom that is not
realized. Vanquishing demons, attaining the way, turning
the wheel of the true teaching and returning to extinction,
all depend on this power. Supernormal powers and their
inconceivable functions, emanating light and expounding
the teaching are all in the act of sitting. Investigation of
zen also is sitting in zazen.

If you want to sit in meditation, first find a quiet place
and lay a thick cushion; do not let wind or smoke, rain or
dew in. Keep a clear place to sit, with enough room for
your knees. Although there were people who sat on diamond seats or boulders in ancient times, they all had sitting cushions. Where you sit should not be light in the
daytime or dark at night; it should be warm in winter and
cool in summer — that's the technique.

Cast off mind, intellect, and consciousnesses, cease recol-
lection, thought, and observation. Don't aim at becoming a
buddha, don't be concerned with right or wrong; value
time, as though saving your head from burning. The
Buddha sat upright, Bodhidharma faced a wall, single-
minded, without any other concerns at all. Shishuang was
like a dead tree, Rujing admonished against sleeping while
sitting; "you can only succeed by just sitting, without
need to make use of burning incense, prostrations, remembrance of buddha names, repentance ceremonies,
reading scriptures or ritual recitations."[12]

Whenever you sit, you should wear a kashaya (kesa) (except during the first and last parts of the night when the daily schedule is not in effect) — don't neglect this. The cushion (twelve inches across, thirty-six in circumference) should not support the whole thighs — it should reach from midthigh to the base of the spine. This is the way the buddhas and patriarchs sat. You may sit in full or half lotus position; the way to sit in full lotus is to put the right foot on the left thigh, then put the left foot on the right thigh. Loosen your clothes and straighten them; next put your right hand on your left foot and your left hand on your right hand, with your thumbs together near the body about the level of your navel. Sit up straight, without leaning to the left or right, front or back. The ears and shoulders, nose and navel, should be aligned. The tongue is kept on the roof of the mouth and the breath should pass through the nose. The mouth should be closed, while the eyes should be open, though not too widely or too slightly.[13] Having attuned your body in this way, breathe deeply through the mouth a couple of times. Next, sitting steady, sway your body seven or eight times, going from larger to smaller movements. Then sit upright and intent.

Now think of what doesn't think —[14] how to think of it? Not thinking. This is the essential method of zazen. You should break directly through afflictions and personally realize enlightenment. When you want to rise from stillness, first put your hands on your knees, sway your body seven or eight times, going from small to larger movements. Open your mouth and breathe out, put your hands on the ground and lightly rise from your seat.

Walk slowly, circling to the right or left. If torpor and sleepiness overcomes you while sitting, always move your body or open your eyes wide; also put your mind on your hairline between your eyebrows. If you still are not wakeful, rub your eyes or body. If that still doesn't wake you up, get up and walk around, always circling to the left.

Once you have gone a hundred steps or so, your sleepiness should have vanished. The way to walk is to take a half step with each breath.[15] You walk as though not walking anywhere, silent and unmoving. If you still don't wake up after walking around like this, either wash your eyes and cool your forehead, or recite the preface to the precepts for bodhisattvas, or some such thing — just find some way not to fall asleep. You should observe that the matter of life and death is a great one, and impermanence is swift — what are you doing sleeping when your eye of the way is not yet clear? If torpor and drowsiness come over you repeatedly, you should pray, "My habits are deepseated, and that is why I am enshrouded by drowsiness — when will my torpor disperse? I pray that the buddhas and enlightened ancestors will be so compassionate as to remove my darkness and misery."

If your mind is scattered, fix your mind on the tip of your nose and lower belly and count your incoming and outgoing breaths. If that doesn't stop your distraction, then bring a saying to mind and keep it in mind to awaken you — for example, "What thing comes thus?" "A dog has no enlightened nature." "When no thought arises, is there still any fault? — Mount Everest!" "What is the meaning of Bodhidharma's coming from the West? — the cypress tree in the garden." Flavorless sayings like this are suitable. If (scattering distraction) still doesn't stop, sit and focus on the point where the breath ends and the eyes close forever, or else where the embryo is not yet conceived and not a single thought is produced; when the twin void[16] suddenly appears, the scattered mind will surely come to rest.

After coming out of stillness, when you carry on your activities without thinking, the present event is the public affair (koan); when you accomplish practice and realization without interfusion,[17] then the public affair is the present happening. That which is before any signs appear, the situation on the other side of the empty aeon, the spiritual capacity of all buddhas and patriarchs, is just this one thing. You should just rest, cease; be cool, passing myriad years as an instant, be cold ashes, a dead tree, an incense burner in an ancient shrine, a piece of white silk. This I pray.

NOTES TO *ZAZEN YOJINKI*

1. In an incident well known in zen circles, the fourteenth patriarch of zen, the Indian master Nagarjuna, once manifested the appearance of a circular figure, like the full moon, where he sat to expound the Dharma; the full moon represents the dharmakaya, or body of reality.

2. The body-mind is represented as being made up of organs and functions corresponding to the four gross elements: earth, water, fire, and air; since early times buddhists in India represented the being to be made up of five clusters: matter, sensation, perception, relational functions (including emotions, judgements, etc.), and consciousness.

3. The five obscurations, or coverings, of the mind in meditation are greed and lust, anger and hatred, folly and delusion, drowsiness, and excitement and regret.

4. This principle is one of the so-called 'four reliances' — to rely on the truth, not the person, which means that anyone can see reality and become enlightened if they go by the truth which is as it is because that is its real nature; it is not a question of human feelings. The other three reliances are to rely on the definitive teaching, not the incomplete teaching, to rely on the meaning and not the words, and to rely on wisdom, not conventional knowledge.

5. The way this is worded it could refer to mystic spells, and/or to silent recitation.

6. This refers to the sixteen stages of mind on the path of insight (darsanamarga) as defined in the Abhidharmakosa: they consist of the tolerance and knowledge of the corresponding truths of suffering, etc., in the 'higher' worlds of form and formlessness (eight more).

7. This refers to the application of the understanding of the twelve links of causality: ignorance, activity, consciousness, name and form, six senses, contact, sensation, desire, attachment, becoming, birth, old age and death. By removing one link the chain can be broken.

8. The six ways of transcendental practice are generosity without conception of giver, receiver, or gift; morality; tolerance; effort; meditation; and wisdom. These are transcendent in that their accomplishment is supposed to involve no sense of subject or object.

9. This refers to blissful and peaceful activities of body, mouth, and mind, and of carrying out vows. According to the Lotus scripture, for the body this means not associating with powerful aristocrats, with sorcerers, with criminals or prostitutes, with butchers, with followers of the vehicles of disciples or self-enlightened ones, desirous thoughts, with hermaphrodites, dangerous places, censured things, or keeping young children as acolytes; once one avoids these ten kinds of people or actions, one is at ease. As far as the mouth is concerned, it means not to indulge in talking about the errors of other people or the scriptures, not to belittle others, not to praise others, not to slander others, and not to be resentful. As far as mind is concerned, it means to avoid flattery, depredation, to avoid scorning those of small actions with one's own grandiose actions, and to avoid contention. Carrying out vows in peace and bliss means using the power of one's vow to rescue all beings to govern oneself.

10. Knowledge of the birthlessness, or nonorigination of all things, was sometimes understood to mean unborn knowledge, or knowledge that is natural and not fabricated. All knowledge is spoken of as general and particular; knowing universal relativity, and knowing the particular relations. Spontaneous knowledge is the knowledge that has no teacher, that doesn't come from without.

11. Tathagata, one who has realized thusness, is an epithet of a buddha.

12. This is a statement of Rujing, Dogen's teacher.

13. Rujing told Dogen that it was all right to close the eyes. A number of recommendations about meditation found in this little work seem to have come from Rujing's teaching.

14.   This could be read think of the unthinkable, or think of what doesn't think; this is a famous saying of Yaoshan, a disciple of Shitou and one of the early ancestors of Soto zen in China.

15.   The foot should be moved a distance equal to the length of the foot. This method of walking in meditation (kinhin) was taught to Dogen by Rujing.

16.   This refers to the voidness of person and things.

17.   Interfusion means nondifferentiation, so not interfusing means differentiation, each thing abiding in its characteristic state — so called 'mountain is mountain, river is river.'

JOKIN'S ESOTERIC SHOBOGENZO

Compiled by Keizan Jokin

CITATION I:

At the assembly on Vulture Peak, before hundreds of thousands of beings, The World-Honored One raised a flower and blinked his eyes. Mahakasyapa broke into a smile. The World-Honored One said, "I have the treasure of the eye of the true teaching, the inconceivable mind of nirvana, the formless adamantine form, and the subtle, ineffable teaching of truth. It is communicated outside of doctrine and does not establish verbal formulations. Today I personally entrust this to Mahakasyapa. Continue to teach in my stead." And he also commended Ananda to transmit it as it is, continuing from successor to successor without letting it be cut off.

JOKIN'S REFLECTIONS:

At the meeting on the holy mountain long ago, all without exception were the circumstance of this "raising a flower" and "smiling." Just as the World-Honored One raised the flower, what was the circumstance? And when Kasyapa smiled, what was the circumstance?

If one perceives it directly, past and present are simultaneously penetrated. One may say, "Without relying on today's situation, how can one speak of last night's dream?"

Later the zen teacher Seiryo of Mt. Kei said, "The World-Honored One had a secret saying — spring lingers on the ancient ford; Kasyapa did not keep it hidden — falling flowers float on the stream."

Also zen master Chikan of Setcho said, "The World-Honored One had a saying, but Kasyapa did not keep it hidden; a night of flowers falling in the rain, water is fragrant throughout the city."

These are models of men of old citing the ancient to illumine the present. I ask you people; at that time, what flower did he raise? What flower did he smile at? Say it straight out now! (Striking a blow) You've stumbled past. Do you understand? There is only one indestructible esoteric body, wholly manifest in the dusts. Look!

CITATION II:

Ananda asked the venerable Kasyapa, "Elder brother, you received the golden robe of The World-Honored One; what else was transmitted besides this?"

Venerable Kasyapa said, "Ananda!"

Ananda responded.

Venerable Kasyapa said, "Take down the monastery banner."

Ananda greatly awakened.

JOKIN'S REFLECTIONS:

Kasyapa calls "Ananda!" Immediately it is perfectly clear; do not harbor any doubt or hesitation. Ananda responds; what sound is this in actuality? If one awakens on the spot, what would there be of any of this?

A man of old said, "Elder brother calls and younger brother replies, revealing the shame of the house; not the province of night and day, this is a separate spring."

As soon as Kasyapa calls Ananda, he is off the track; the immediate reply is off the track. At this very moment, how do you understand?

(Striking) What season is this? Do you understand? It's right at hand; immediately concentrate your eye and see. Investigate!

CITATION III:

Emperor Bu of Ryo asked the great master Bodhidharma, "What is the highest meaning of the holy truths?"

The great teacher said, "Empty; nothing is holy."

The Emperor said, "Who is replying to me?"

The great teacher said, "I don't know."

The Emperor did not understand.

JOKIN'S REFLECTIONS:

"Empty; nothing is holy" does not establish real or provisional, does not discuss doctrine or contemplation. Even the buddhas of the three times cannot see it; even the six generations of patriarchs could not transmit it. This is the time when the land is quiet.

And it was said, "Who is replying to me?" A good scene, but do you see? The great teacher said, "I don't know." Why does he not know? Not knowing is the public affair that is now manifest. As for the "manifestation," mountains are really mountains, rivers are really rivers. Wrong! Mountains cannot know mountains, rivers cannot know rivers. Like so the Whole Body manifests; there is no further entry point.

And ultimately? "I only allow The Old Barbarian's knowledge: I do not allow his understanding." Investigate!

CITATION IV:

A monk asked zen master Gyoshi of Seigen, "What work does not fall into stages?"

The master said, "Even the holy truths are not practiced."

The monk bowed.

JOKIN'S REFLECTIONS:

The place clear, the time obvious, there are no stages or tracks. Leave it to fate, leave it to fate, always like this.

Sekito made a verse in praise of Yakusan:

> *Though we've been dwelling together, I don't know*
> *   his name;*
> *Abandoned to fate, we go along as ever.*

> *Even the great sages since the remote past do not*
> *know him;*
> *How could the later rabble understand him?*

If you would understand the words, "Even the noble truths are not carried out," you should seek out the intent of this verse.

Ultimately, how is it? "A patchrobed monk sits with shrouded head, not knowing aught of cool or warmth." Investigate!

CITATION V:

Our ancestor, the great teacher Gohon of Tozan, asked Ungan, "Who can hear inanimate objects preaching the Dharma?"

Ungan said, "The inanimate can hear."

Tozan said, "Why do I not hear?"

Ungan raised his whisk and said, "Do you hear?"

Tozan said, "I do not hear."

Ungan said, "You do not even hear my preaching; how could you hear the preaching of the inanimate?"

Tozan thereupon had an insight; he then chanted a verse:

> *Wonderful! Wonderful!*
> *The sermon of the inanimate is inconceivable:*
> *If one uses the ears to hear, it will be after all*
> *impossible to understand;*
> *Only by hearing with the eyes can one know.*

JOKIN'S REFLECTIONS:

This is the time of great awakening and thorough penetration. If you hear Mount An discussing wisdom, how could you doubt Mount Ju's talk of true suchness? The pillar and the lamp are also thus.

At the time that the inanimate preach the Dharma, what are the circumstances? If you understand, then communities are preaching, beings are preaching, all in the three times are simultaneously preaching. They are always preaching, clearly preaching, without pause.

Layman Toba studied with Shogaku and gained entry into the way, whereupon he expressed his inner experience:

> The sound of the valley is an immense tongue;
> Is not the color of the mountains the pure body?
> Since evening, eighty-four thousand verses —
> How could I recite them to others?

Already he has cited them all. Also he said,

> The valley sound; an immense tongue:
> The mountain colors; a pure body.
> Eighty-four thousand verses;
> Later I recite them to others.

Before he said, "How to express them to others?" Here he says, "I express them to others." Are these the same or different? If one can hear the content of the sermon of the inanimate, it rests with him; where does he not express to others?

Tell me, how is it when one hears it expressed to people? Ungan and Tozan, Shogaku and Toba, have their nostrils pierced all at once. But do you understand? (Silence) Speechless speech is true speech. Investigate!

CITATION VI:

Zen master Hakuun Doju asked a monk, "'Speaking, silent, not speaking, not silent; wholly so, wholly not so' — how do you reply?" The monk had no answer. The master then hit him.

JOKIN'S REFLECTIONS:

Speech, silence, motion, stillness; wholly so, wholly not so. Outside this group, in what manner could one respond? The monk did not reply — "who knows the law fears it." After all, he has realized a little bit. As the first blow of the staff, the effort was not made in vain.

I ask you people, when the six senses are inoperative and the seven consciousnesses are not present, what will you use to answer? Why do you not bow and leave?

Kyogen's story of 'up in a tree' may also be seen in the same way as the phrase beyond the six propositions. If you can express the matter of the tree, then you understand the single phrase beyond the six propositions.

But say; without setting up either 'the tree top' or 'that which is beyond the six propositions,' coming directly to this point here, how will you turn around and show some life? (striking) Look!

(Note on Kyogen's story: he said, "Suppose a man climbs a tree and is holding on to a branch with his mouth, his hands not holding any limb, his feet not standing on the trunk: under the tree there is someone who asks about the reason why Bodhidharma came from the West; if (the man in the tree) doesn't answer, he is ignoring the question, but if he does answer, he still loses his body and life. At this moment, how would you answer?" The 'six propositions' are speech, silence, etc., as mentioned in the citation.)

CITATION VII:

Zen master Goso asked a monk, "The girl Sei split her spirit; which one is real?" The monk had no reply.

JOKIN'S REFLECTIONS:

This is the situation which is beyond the reach of 'lord and vassal,' 'biased and true.' It is not the wonderful principle of the zen way or of the buddhist teaching.

If one is already two, how could they be one? If you say the two are one, why are there two? Try to say which is real.

Shakyamuni Buddha manifests a hundred-thousand million emanation bodies; the bodhisattva Avalokitesvara is endowed with so many hands and eyes: are they the same or different?

Thus it is said, "Above to the summit of the heavens, below to the deepest hells, all is as yellow gold." Thus there are no signs of self and others, of society and individual. Such is this situation; which is Shakyamuni, which is Avalokitesvara?

Also, Manjusri spent summer retreat in the wineshops, brothels, and butcher shops: Kasyapa, wanting to drive him away, reached for him with a staff when suddenly he saw hundreds of millions of billions of Manjusris. Shakyamuni said, "Kasyapa, which Manjusri would you drive out?" Kasyapa had no reply. This is the same situation: which is Manjusri? Which is Kasyapa? Which is the real one? Try to say.

There's an echo in Shakyamuni's words when he says, "Which Manjusri would you drive out?" If you can understand this saying, then you should be able to see the saying "Sei split her spirit." Goso's "Debt of gratitude to the elixir of eternal life" is based on this saying.

Therefore it is said, "Before me, no you; here, no me." Why is it like this? Because mind and body are one suchness. A living man's tongue is a dead man's mouth; a dead man walks on a living man's road. At this moment it is indescribably perfect; it is not concealing or revealing. Illumining the whole body, alive and unconstrained; the great function is not in the image of man — behold its visage, clearly manifest; there is no buddha way, no patriarchal path. Knowledge of all knowledge, pure and clear, absolutely unique, it is without duality and without separation, because it has no gap.

Ultimately how is it? The girl Sei split her spirit; which is the real one? Investigate!

(Note: this koan refers to the story of a young woman named Sei who took to a sickbed when her betrothed went away without her. As her betrothed was going, however, he saw Sei coming after him; thus reunited, they spent five years together before the man decided to return. When they got back, the man found that Sei had been seen lying on her sickbed for these five years: when he brought the 'Sei' he had been living with to the sickbed where the pining 'Sei' lay, the two 'Sei's merged into one. Goso asks, "Which is the real one?")

CITATION VIII:

The zen master Tokusan Senkan one day left the hall carrying his bowl. Seppo saw him and said, "Old man, the bell has not yet rung, the drum not yet sounded; where are you going with your bowl?"

Tokusan lowered his head and returned to his abbot's quarters.

Seppo brought this up to Ganto, who said, "That Tokusan has after all not yet understood the last word."

Tokusan had his attendant summon Ganto, whom he asked, "You do not agree with this old monk?"

Ganto silently expressed his meaning; Tokusan said nothing.

JOKIN'S REFLECTIONS:

Tokusan just accepts the flow, being as is. Ganto and Seppo scatter rubbish in the eye; playing at being adept, they turn out inept.

Tokusan lowered his head and returned to his abbot's room; what contrivance is there in this? If you try to approach it in terms of inside and outside, dependent and true, subject and object, or guest and host, you have not even seen it in dreams. Carrying the bowl, lowering the head, returning to the room — what ease or difficulty is there?

Seppo once said to his congregation, "We meet at the inn in Bo province, we meet at the Raven Peak, we meet in front of the monks' hall." Hofuku asked Gacho, "I do not ask about the monks' hall; as for the inn in Bo province or the Raven Peak, where do we meet?" Gacho ran hurriedly back to his abbot's quarters; Hofuku thereupon went into the monks' hall. This is the time. What doctrine is this?

Where there is not the slightest breath, if you can understand this story, then you will see the story about Tokusan carrying his bowl.

Ultimately how is it? Be uniformly equanimous; of itself it disappears without a trace.

Also I say 'Wrong!" There is still the final word. How do you see it? Investigate!

CITATION IX:

Zen master Gyozan Ejaku was asked by a monk, "Can the Dharma-body also expound the Dharma?"

Gyozan said, "I cannot expound it, but there is another who can."

The monk said, "Where is the one who expounds the Dharma?"

Gyozan pushed forward a pillow.

Isan (Gyozan's teacher) heard of this and remarked, "Mr. Ejaku is bringing out the action of a sword."

JOKIN'S REFLECTIONS:

This monk was not anxious for his life under the sword; he brought up a question. and Gyozan didn't slip with his sword — he cut off the man's head before he knew it.

Just when he pushes the pillow forward, there is a unique subtlety; can it be considered the one who replies? Or can it be considered a pillow? Can it be considered the act of pushing forward? Here, how will you understand? I push forth a cushion; do you people really see? (Making a whistling sound) Like this! Investigate!

CITATION X:

Zen master Kassan Zenne was asked by a monk, "What is the way?"

Kassan said, "The sun floods the eye; not a fleck of cloud for ten thousands miles."

The monk said, "I do not understand."

Kassan said, "In the clear water, the wandering fish deludes itself."

135

JOKIN'S REFLECTIONS:

The One Great Matter has always been manifest; do not seek enlightenment, for fundamentally there is no illusion. Lucid, without obscurity, everywhere perfectly obvious; why do you not understand? People of today are as if riding an ox in search of an ox.

A monk asked Haryo, "What is the way?" Haryo said, "A clear-eyed man falls into a well." If the eye is clear, one should see the road and go directly on; why fall into a well? If you understand this story, then you will see the koan saying "In the clear water, the meandering fish deludes itself."

Do you understand? The sky is clear, there is no rain; why do you not see the sun and moon? Investigate!

I have cited ten examples of the acts of the ancient worthies; pass through them one by one.

The first, the story of raising the flower and smiling, is the setting of the one great concern of all buddhas of the three times.

The second, the story of the banner before the monastery, is the model of the enlightenment of all the patriarchs.

The third, the story of emptiness and not knowing, is the subtlety which the patriarchs and buddhas neither transmit nor receive.

The fourth, the story of not even practicing the holy truths, is the point to which the historical patriarchs actually attained.

The fifth, the story of the sermon of the inanimate, is the beginning of our ancestor's understanding mind and awakening to the way.

The sixth, the story of one expression outside of the six propositions, is that which all monks in the world can neither swallow nor spit out.

The seventh, the girl Sei separating her spirit, is the power of intrepid zeal of all buddhas and all patriarchs.

The eighth, leaving the hall with bowl in hand, is the ancient's way of letting go and accepting the flow.

The ninth, the story of the pillow, is the ancient worthies' method of not grabbing the sword and cutting the hand.

The tenth, the story of not understanding the way, is the aspect of the ancients extending their hands to save those enshrouded by ignorance.

Soseki of Soji

The zen master's initiatory name was Soseki; he was styled Gazan. He was from Noto prefecture, and his lay surname was Minamoto; he was a descendant of the great councillor Reizei. His mind was exceptionally keen, and his clear countenance was extraordinary.

As a youth he gave up lay life and climbed right up to Mount Hiei, where he set up an altar and received the precepts. He often went to lectures and studied thoroughly the essentials of the school of Tendai. When he happened to meet zen master Keizan at Daijo monastery, Keizan saw at once that he was a vessel of truth, so he said to him, "A fine vessel of dharma; why don't you change your vestments and investigate zen?" The master Gazan said, "I have a mother and I fear she would lack support (if I did so)." Keizan said, "In ancient times Sanavasa gave up a whole continent to enter our school; how can you neglect the way of the greatest teaching for a petty mundane duty?" Then he took off his outer robe and gave it to Gazan, who joyfully accepted it with a bow.

Then he went along with Keizan when he moved to Soji monastery. He was wholehearted and sincere at all times, never once straying. One day when Keizan got up in the hall to speak, the master Gazan came forward from the assembly and asked, "Why is it hard to speak of the place where not a breath enters?" Keizan said, "Even speaking of it does not say it." The master had a flash of insight; as he was about to open his mouth, Keizan said, "Wrong." Scolded, Gazan withdrew; after this his spirit of determination soared far beyond that of ordinary people. One night as Keizan was enjoying the moon along with Gazan, he said, "Do you know that there are two moons?" Gazan said, "No." Keizan said, "If you don't know there are two moons,* you are not a seedling of the To succession."

At this the master increased his determination and sat crosslegged like an iron pole for years. One day as Keizan passed through the hall he said, "'Sometimes it is right to have Him raise his eyebrows and blink his eyes; sometimes it is right not to have Him raise his eyebrows and blink his eyes.'"** At these words the master Gazan was greatly enlightened. Then with full ceremony he expressed his understanding. Keizan agreed with him and said, "After the ancients had gotten the message, they went north and south, polishing and chipping day and night, never complacent or self-conceited. From today you should go call on (the teachers) in other places."

Gazan bowed and took his leave that very day. At all the monasteries he visited he distinguished the dragons from the snakes.† After a long time of this he eventually returned to look in on Keizan. Keizan welcomed him joyfully and said, "Today you finally can be a seedling of the To succession." The master Gazan covered his ears.

Keizan said, "I am getting feeble and am depending on a hand from you to hold up a broken sand bowl;" then he transmitted the teaching to him. After the master had received it, he led the community at Soji. The monastery regulations were fully developed, modeled on the strict rules of Tiantong. Before long people from all walks of life came like clouds. Always surrounded by thousands of people, Gazan greatly expounded Soto zen.

* The moon is the symbol of reality. Traditionally 'middle path' buddhism provisionally distinguishes two levels of reality, conventional (social) and ultimate ('emptiness').

** This is a saying of Shitou.

† Dragons are great meditation adepts; snakes are those that resemble 'dragons' but aren't really; that is, Gazan saw who were the genuine knowers and who were the imitations.

Gazan Soseki had twenty-five enlightened disciples to whom he transmitted the Dharma; each spread the teaching in one region, and the influence of the school spread all over the country. At the end of his life he had Taigen inherit his seat, and also entrusted Tsugen with the sceptre of authority of the school. After he had imparted his last instruction to his various disciples Mutan, Daitetsu, Hobo, and the rest, he rang the bell, chanted a verse, and died.

His verse said,

> *Skin and flesh together*
> *Ninety one years.*
> *Since night, as of old,*
> *I lie in the yellow springs of death.*

Jakurei of Yotaku

The zen master's initiatory name was Jakurei; he was styled Tsugen. He was from Kyoto. He was orphaned as a child and was raised by his grandmother. He saw that he was physically unfit for worldly occupations, and climbed Mount Hiei to have his head shaved. His mind and appearance were outstanding and brilliant; he could understand scriptures at a glance. He deeply cultivated and refined the teachings (of Tendai buddhism) of cessation and insight. He had some doubt and set his mind on that which is beyond the teachings; so he left (Hiei) and called on zen master Gazan at Soji.

Gazan asked, "Where have you come from?" He said, "Mount Hiei." Gazan said, "What do you seek?" He said, "I have doubted the teaching of cessation and insight for a long time." Gazan said, "Don't indulge in imagination!" Tsugen's feeling of doubt flared up all the more, to the point where he forgot about eating and sleeping. Gazan knew he was a vessel of Dharma, and questioned him closely about the saying about shedding body and mind.

One morning the master Tsugen was suddenly enlightened and said, "Old teacher, don't fool people!" Gazan said, "What truth have you seen?" He said, "Riding backwards on the buddha shrine, going out the main gate." Gazan agreed with this. After that Tsugen studied with Gazan for a very long time and understood all the stories of past and present.

When the master Tsugen received the robe symbolizing the faith, he expounded the teaching at Yotaku and Ryusen monasteries; his fame in the way was honored beyond the seas, and crowds of people came and went ceaselessly. At that time the emperor Goenju of the Oan era sent down an edict granting Tsugen authority over the whole school throughout the land; because of this, the standards of Soto zen were strict everywhere.

The master was most high minded and didn't speak with people. He always stayed in one room and forgot all about society. One day he had a slight illness; he rang the bell and told the assembly, then admonished them, "People, you should end all entanglements and concentrate on understanding your own affair. On the other side, throw away useless words and letters; on this side, slough off evanescent honor and profit — wherever you are, be clean and free and you may be true seedlings of the To succession. Otherwise, you are not my disciples."

He asked for a brush and wrote a verse saying,

> Coming and going in this world,
> A full seventy years;
> Here where I turn around,
> My feet tread upon the heavens.

Having written this, he died sitting peacefully.

Emyo of Saijo

The zen master's initiatory name was Emyo; he was styled Ryoan. He was from Sagami prefecture. When he was young he left the world and went to Kencho monastery. He was great by nature and people who saw him cowered. It came to pass that he thought to himself, "In the investigation of zen, if one does not meet an enlightened teacher, one may get sidetracked and waste effort and trouble. I hear zen master Tsugen, the sixth generation of Eihei, has the power to help people pull out the nails and stakes. Days and months fly by; why stick by a stump* and remain in a little byway?" So he set out to Yotaku.

Tsugen's manner of teaching was extremely remote and inaccessible; a lot of people who came were not allowed to enter his room, and often had to "stay with their hats on" for years. When the master Ryoan first got there, Tsugen asked, "Where have you come from?" He said, "Sagami." Tsugen said, "How far was the journey?" He said, "Over three hundred miles." Tsugen said, "How many sandals did you wear out?" He said, "I lost count." Tsugen hit him on the head and said, "I don't keep any rice bags like this around here." The master was greatly enlightened at these words and immediately expressed his understanding in verse. Tsugen gave him the seal of recognition and allowed him to enter the room. The whole community was amazed.

* This refers to a well known story of a man who saw a rabbit run into a stump and die, so he waited by the stump to catch another rabbit; this exemplifies someone who clings to a method or teaching, especially to verbal formulations, in hopes of attaining enlightenment.

The next day Tsugen said in the teaching hall, "There is an iron-nose ox here who entered the room last night and had it out with this old monk." Then he got down from the teaching seat and put master Ryoan in the senior monk's seat. After a long time in that position, Ryoan received the robe of faith and eventually returned to Sagami. He began to teach at Saijo, and produced two people of like mind, Taiko and Mukyoku, and the influence of the Soto school flourished in eastern Japan.

Ryoan used to say to the community, "Zen folk, if you want to illumine your selves, you must succeed in doing so in the midst of all kinds of confusion and upsets; don't make the mistake of sitting dead in the cold ashes of a withered tree. When I was in the community of my late teacher, I lost my nostrils at the blow of a staff and have not found them to this day."

Myoshu of Daiji

The zen master's initiatory name was Myoshu, he was styled Taiko; there is no record of his family name. He first called on Ryoan Emyo at Saijo and asked, "What is an entry for the student?" Emyo said, "Come here." The moment Taiko approached, Emyo grabbed him and pushed him away, saying, "There is no way of entry for you here." As Taiko got up, the feeling of doubt suddenly arose; day or night he couldn't put it off.

Emyo knew secretly that Taiko was a vessel of dharma, and subsequently drove him out of the temple on the pretext that he had broken the rules. Taiko felt no resentment, but secretly borrowed a room near the monastery and hid there. For six years he was never forgiven, and just sat facing a wall day and night. His meditation work became increasingly refined, till he got to the point of forgetting to sleep or eat. One day as he stood beside a cowpen he suddenly had an insight; he immediately went to the abbot's quarters with full ceremony. Emyo hollered at him, "Who gave you permission to come inside the temple?" He said, "Here an entry is wide open." Emyo laughed and said, "A thief has broken down my door." The master bowed.

Thereafter the master Taiko served as Emyo's personal attendant, going deeper into the mystery every day. Late in life he began to teach at Daiji monastery, and before long his fame spread far and wide. The master was austere with the community, and never carelessly wasted even a cup of water. He cooked rice and sorted vegetables himself — people saw he had the will to lead a community, and they stayed there; there were never less than a thousand people surrounding his teaching seat.

Eventually Taiko "distributed the wellspring" of zen to fill twelve streams. On one occasion when he had a slight illness he beat the drum to call the community. When everyone had assembled, the master said, "My teaching is come to an end; I am making a bequest to you;" then he raised his staff, shouted once and died standing.

Sosan of Saisho

The zen master's initiatory name was Sosan; he was styled Goho. It is not known where he was born. As a man he was naturally good and wise and whenever he spoke it was something unusual. When he was fifteen he was sincerely bent on investigating zen; at that time he used to visit zen master Taiko at Daiji monastery; every time he asked about the great matter, but Taiko did not reply at all — he only said, "Understand on your own." For six or seven years he did not teach him anything particular.

One morning as the master was at home sweeping up, his broom hit a rock and broke; he suddenly had insight. He went directly to tell Taiko about it, and Taiko acknowledged it. Subsequently Goho gave up lay life and was ordained, and served as the rice cooker. He was always pure and true, and never lay down.

One morning as Taiko passed by the kitchen and saw the master washing rice and putting it in the pot he asked, "The pot is made of iron, the rice is made of grain; what does this show?"* The master said, "Let the pot be made of iron, let the rice be made of grain," then he splashed water on the ground. Taiko deeply approved of him, and gave him the seal of recognition, predicting, "Our school will prosper with you; do not speak easily." Then he gave him the robe of faith, which the master accepted with bowed head and left.

Later Goho began to teach at Saisho and greatly expounded the Soto school. He said, "The bamboo of the southern groves, the wood of the northern lands; the vegetables of the east garden, the wheat of the west field; these are the real livelihood of patchrobed monks; how do you people understand yourselves?" After a long pause he said, "Just stretch out your legs on the long beach and sleep in peace; just have no concerns at all. If you are fellows who talk in your sleep with your eyes open, I'll give you thirty blows of the staff." Then Unshu came forward from the assembly and said, "You have already tasted a score of blows, teacher!" The master laughed aloud and got down from his seat.

* 'what' here is literally 'what side,' meaning 'this side,' the mundane, or 'that side,' the transcendental.

Soryu of Kogon

The zen master's initiatory name was Soryu; he was styled Unshu. He was from Izumo, and his family had been Shinto priests for generations and were wealthy. Once when he was a boy he happened to see a frog die as he crossed by a field with his father; he asked, "Why can't the frog jump?" His father said, "It's dead." He said, "Do people also die?" His father said, "Yes." He said, "How can it be avoided?" His father said, "I have heard that one who understands buddhism can escape it." He said, "I want to understand buddhism; how can I do so?" His father considered him unusual and thought that the boy was not ordinary and his determination could not be changed, so he put him in Gakuen temple and had him leave home and society (and become a monk).

Before he had reached the age of fifteen he determined to study zen; he travelled all over seeking certainty. Finally he called on master Sosan at Saisho; his expression of his state and his actions were fitting, and Sosan granted him the position of second-ranked monk and secretary. He studied with Sosan for years and intimately attained the mind seal. Later in life he began to teach at Kogan monastery; the true line of the To school continued unerring.

One evening he called his disciple Bun'ei to come to his room and instructed him, "Our path is transmitted by way of four kinds of guest and host: sometimes absolute, sometimes relative; sometimes both absolute and relative are illumined together, and sometimes absolute and relative both disappear." Then he poked the air with his finger and said, "This point is neither relative nor absolute; the buddhas and patriarchs since time immemorial cannot grasp it. Later on you will have broken thatch to cover your head; don't accept people too easily. I won't be around long." Then be bequeathed to him the robe and the teaching, wrote a verse, announced his illness and died after three days.

Bun'ei of Tennei

The zen master's initiatory name was Bun'ei; he was styled Ikke. He first called on zen master Unshu at Kogan; as soon as Unshu saw him, he knew in himself that he was a vessel of Dharma. Unshu sent Bun'ei to work as cook. The master Bun'ei was completely earnest in his daily activities. One day as Unshu passed by the kitchen he encountered the master sorting vegetables by himself. Unshu said, "How long have you been here?" He said, "Over a year." Unshu said, "Outside of sorting vegetables and washing rice, what work do you do?" He said, "I work at meditation." Unshu said, "What is the aim of your meditation?" He said, "I want to become a buddha." Unshu said, "What is the use of being a buddha?" Bun'ei was stirred up by this; he increased in determination and didn't sleep day or night.

Once it happened that when Unshu was in the teaching hall a monk asked, "What is the place where a patchrobed monk comes forth?" Unshu said, "Blow on willow fuzz and hairballs fly; when the rain hits the flowers, yellow butterflies fly." The master Bun'ei, standing by, was set free. That evening he went to the abbot's quarters in full ceremony; Unshu said, "The vegetable picker has finished

147

with the great matter." The master bowed. After this he attended Unshu personally, continuing to inquire with utmost concentration.

When Unshu finally died, the master began to teach at Tennei. A monk came to call and asked, "What is the master's family style?" The master said, "On the meditating shadow the shoulders are as thin as bamboo; the spirit of the way is grand and solitary as a pine." The monk asked, "Suppose a guest comes; then what?" He said, "The tea is warm in the broken pot — you should drink it; the fragrance is gone from the cold oven — I am tired of cooking."

The master Bun'ei was a simple and direct man and didn't like ostentation; it was impossible to be familiar with him.

Koken of Bansho

The zen master's initiatory name was Koken; he was styled Muteki. It is not known where he was from. He happened to visit zen master Bun'ei at Tennei; Bun'ei liked the master's simplicity and genuine sincerity. Their words and actions met together like a needle and a seed.* The master then stayed and went back to the hall; he wrapped up his staff and bowl himself, hung them high on the wall and

---

* The image of needle and seed meeting is often used for the rare occasion of meeting of true master and true disciple.

sat. Except for meals of gruel and rice at dawn and midday, and for answering the calls of nature, he never left his seat. Winter and summer alike he only wore a single robe; even in severe cold and muggy heat he never put on anything more or took anything off. He stayed for twenty years as though it were but a single day.

One evening Bun'ei called the master to come to him; he raised the robe of the teaching and said, "This was old Unshu's; I received it there by sorting vegetables and washing rice for the community. Now I am pressed for time and want to impart it to you; can I?" He said, "I am not such a man." Bun'ei said, "I esteem your not being such a man. Go away this very day, to where there are no tracks, pick out a man of the way and transmit it to the succeeding generation — do not let our teaching be cut off." Then he handed it over; the master assented.

After that Koken built a hut at the foot of Mount Fuji and lived there; he called it Bansho, "Myriad Pines." He shut off the road to the world and didn't cross the threshold of the gate for another twenty years. He wrote a poem,

> Since coming to this reed hut
> I have never looked for human hearths.
> At noon I gather forest fruits,
> In the evening I boil spring water.
> Sewing clouds together, my cold patchwork robe is
>   thick;
> Gathering leaves, my old seat is tranquil.
> The green and yellow colors beyond the eaves
> Remind me of the passing year.

Late in life, after he entrusted the teaching to Eiko, he burned his hut and went away to no one knows where.

Eiko of Choan

The zen master's initiatory name was Eiko; he called himself Jutenmin. He was from Bungo prefecture. He left society as a youth and always concentrated on the matter pertaining to his own self. When he was fifteen he went traveling; at every monastery he went to he was praised and considered extraordinary. He called on over thirty teachers and understood the manner and character of all of them.

One day as he was passing through Suruga on his travels he happened to hear that zen master Koken was living in a hut below Mount Fuji. The master thought, "A monk travels in order to meet an enlightened teacher; why hesitate to go seek him out?" So he went looking for Koken, traveling ten difficult miles over the banks of rushing streams and past withered tree crags, finally reaching him.

When Koken saw Eiko arrive, he sat facing the wall in meditation. The master Eiko went up behind him, bowed and pleaded, "A disciple has come ten miles expecially to pay obeisance to you, teacher; please be so compassionate as to face me." Koken didn't pay attention to him. The master said, "If you don't face me, I'll beat you to death." Koken still didn't turn around; the master Eiko knew he was a real man of knowledge. Then he thought up a ploy; he put his bundle under his arm and left — but once he was outside the gate he secretly returned and silently watched from behind the fence for Koken to come out of stillness. Koken, not realizing he had fallen for Eiko's scheme, eventually got up and went out; Eiko suddenly came out from behind the fence, whereat Koken, startled, rushed back inside. Eiko followed him and asked, "What is buddhism in the mountains?" Koken said, "From the beginning of the valley stream to the end, water is still water; north of the hut, south of the hut, mountains are mountains." Eiko believed and submitted to him without reservation; he bowed with full ceremony and pledged to wait on Koken, drawing water and gathering fruit. Day and night he served him closely for twelve years.

One day Koken said to Eiko, "I have a patchwork robe, coming apart at the seams, which weighs a thousand pounds; if you want to bear it, you must use all your strength in your arm. I am going; take it away." Then he gave the robe to Eiko. The master Eiko tearfully accepted it with a bow. Late in life, because of the insistent request of donors, he began to teach at Choan; crowds of people came to him from all over.

Eiko always taught the community, "In investigating zen it is necessary to meet an enlightened teacher; once you meet an enlightened teacher, you must focus your mind undividedly for months and years. If you casually wear out sandals traveling over river and lake, when will you ever be done?"

Gensaku of Tocho

The zen master's initiatory name was Gensaku; he was styled Ryoshu. Nither the circumstances of his birth nor his early studies are recorded. When he was traveling he heard of zen master Eiko's fame in the way and went specially to call on him. Eiko assigned him to attend to (Eiko's) cloth and bowl; he always worked earnestly and investigated thoroughly and carefully. One day Eiko tested him with the saying about the ox going through the window lattice;* the master was at a loss — Eiko said, "If you study zen in this way, you're just wasting food money." At this the master aroused his determination; he was stirred up all the time and his mind was uneasy — so he went before the buddha image and vowed, "As long as I have not clarified the great matter, I will not eat or drink at all." Nothing had touched his lips for over ten days when he happened to hear a fellow work monk reading the record of Dogen's sayings at Eihei; when he got to the point where it says, "the red heart bared entirely, who can know? What a laugh, the lad on the way to Huangmei,"** he was suddenly greatly enlightened.

After that he never left Eiko's side and eventually succeeded to the seat at Choan, where the whole community gladly submitted to him. He was respected all over in his time for his practice of the way.

The master said, "In one there are many, in two there is no duality — how do you reckon the phrase in between? Last year was austere, with neither rice nor wheat; this year is rich with vegetables and fruit."

Later he opened Tocho monastery and moved there; the patrons and the community submitted to him just as when he was at Choan.

* Wuzu Fayan said, "It is like an ox going through a window lattice; his head, horns, and feet have all passed through — why can't the tail also pass?" This famous koan is in the *Mumonkan*.

** The lad going to Huangmei is Huineng, the future sixth patriarch of zen in China on his way north to Huangmei to see the fifth patriarch Hongren.

Zenban of Ankoku

The zen master's initiatory name was Zenban; he was styled Ten'o. He was born in the Unno clan in Shimano. When he was young he was gentle and kind, always smiling. He was never heard to cry, but he never spoke, either; people in his village thought he was mute. He first spoke when he happened to see an image of a buddha. His parents jumped for joy; they asked him, "You can speak! Why have you been silent all these years?" He said, "As I heard ordinary converations, it was mostly common vulgarities; that's why I didn't speak." His parents were startled and thought he was strange; eventually they allowed him to leave home.

While he was travelling to study zen, everyone esteemed him as having innate virtue. When he called on zen master Gensaku at Choan, as soon as Gensaku saw him he knew he had innate knowledge and didn't need a word of examination — he assigned him to the senior seat.

One evening Gensaku summoned the master and said, "I am sick, unable to rise; I transmit this misfortune to you," then he gave him the robe and died. The master could not but succeed to the seat and dwell there, but he never assumed his proper position ('the absolute state') as abbot; he placed a portrait of his late teacher Gensaku in the abbot's quarters and paid respects to it morning and evening along with the community for a full year. Because of this the community of followers really submitted to him.

Visitors came all the time. The master always thought of giving up temple affairs and eventually entrusted the seat to Enshu and left. Late in life he opened up Ankoku as a place to finish out his old age; here he wrote,

> I have longed to hide for ten years;
> Finally weaving a reed hut, I can meditate in peace.

153

Opening the stove, I put a little damp wood in the
fire;
Don't mistakenly lift the blind and let my smoke
out.

Shutan of Kosho

The zen master's initiatory name was Shutan; he was
styled Eshu. As a youth he had his head shaved by zen
master Gensaku at Choan and served him as a teacher.
After Gensaku died, he next served as personal attendant
to Ten'o, taking care of his robes and bowl. He attended
these two teachers for over thirty years in all, and delved
deeply into the matter of his own self; Ten'o always called
him a real leaver of home.

Once as Ten'o was talking over tea he said to the group,
"Buddhism is like a born enemy; there's no way for you to
approach. If there is a fellow here who can come forth and
tie up the enemy's staff, I will give him a stinking loincloth and let him be abbot." The master Eshu came forward and said, "Everyone has the mettle to challenge the
heavens, but it's better to go the way of the enlightened
ones." Then be brushed out his sleeves and left. Ten'o
pointed around and said, "Without a determination such
as this, how could anyone get my stinking loincloth?"

After a long time Eshu received the teaching and appeared in the world at Choan. The master was a most solemn and upright man; he was so stern it was impossible
to be familiar with him. If anyone broke the rules of the
temple, he would forcibly eject them. He once said, "My

former teacher had me be the master of this temple; how could I dare take it easy?" Those who heard him were scared.

Later in life he entrusted the teaching to Zokuo and retired to the western hall."* Finally he opened Kosho temple, where the monastic standards were modeled on those of Choan.

* The western hall is the traditional abode of the retired abbot.

Soden of Ryuko

The zen master's initiatory name was Soden; he was styled Zokuo. He was from Mutsu prefecture, but his name, ordination and early studies are not known. He was a strong and direct man, extremely vulgar in speech and action; at all the monasteries he went to he was called Rustic Den. He was extremely brilliant and very good at poetry, but no one knew this.

One day as he was traveling through Kamakura he happened to go to Kencho monastery. The followers there, seeing the master's rustic crudeness, laughed and made fun of him, but he sung aloud happily, as if no one were there. Someone casually composed a verse and showed it to the master; as soon as he read it the master knew the phrasing was adequate but the pure essence was not yet ripe. Then he replied with three verses of his own, and everyone was so startled they couldn't even clap in appreciation; he got up and left them.

Later he called on zen master Shutan at Choan. Shutan tested him with the story, "A monk asked Yunmen, 'When one doesn't produce a single thought, is there any fault or not?' Yunmen said, 'Mount Everest!'" and had the master say something about it. The master tried seven or eight comments, but Shutan didn't agree. Shutan admonished him, "The way of enlightenment is beyond the reach of discrimination and emotion; how can it admit of your intellectual calculations or your fancy replies? If you really want to understand this great matter, you can only do so if you put down what you have learned by your brilliance."

The master now increased his determination, burned all his notebooks of writings he had studied before, and engaged in investigation with utmost concentration. After two months he reached the point where he was not aware of his hands moving or feet walking. One night while he was walking in the hall, he bumped his head on a pillar and was suddenly enlightened. He rushed right to the abbot's quarters; Shutan said, "Rustic Den, your great task is done." The master bowed.

After he had become an abbot, he said to his community, "Since I bumped my head on a pillar in my late teacher's community, the pain has not stopped, even now." Later he opened Ryuko and Saifuku temples, and produced two collateral branches of the teaching.

Yohan of Choan

The zen master's initiatory name was Yohan; he was styled Goten. He came from a Kazusa family of the Taira clan. He was naturally pure and unattached, uninvolved in the ordinary world. He always sat peacefully by the window, relaxed and at ease. His parents took him to a local buddhist temple and let him leave home.

He studied and mastered the essentials of the exoteric and esoteric schools; his thought and conversation was extremely profound and he was esteemed everywhere for his lectures on the scriptures. One day he met a zen man who questioned him closely about meaning, whereupon he repented and shifted his mind to zen meditation. Eventually he went traveling around and entered Rinzai and Soto zen monasteries.

He called on over one hundred zen teachers in all, before he finally called on Zokuo at Choan. As Zokuo saw the master entering the door, he drove him out with loud shouts. The master stumbled and fell; as soon as he stood up, he was suddenly vastly and greatly enlightened. Thereupon he spoke a verse;

> One shout of the void
> And suddenly a corpse revives;
> A patchrobed monk's gate of entry
> Penetrates everywhere.

Zokuo gave him the seal of recognition; thenceforth he changed his robe and followed Zokuo like a shadow or an echo for seventeen years, day by day going into the mysterious profundity.

Later, when Zokuo moved to Ryuko, the old worthies at the temple, along with the patrons, asked the master to succeed Zokuo at Choan; the master declined, saying he was not yet refined enough. When they insisted again and again, he finally assented; those who have the will to lead a group always have the ability to transcend the teacher. The master said in the hall, "A golden hen lays an iron egg; a stone cow embraces a jade calf — here there is some happening, but how many people can discover their real potential?"

Shinryu of Choan

The zen master's initiatory name was Shinryu; he called himself Big Cloud. No one knew where he came from. He was a high minded man, given to grandiose talk; everywhere he went he was disliked and ousted by the groups there. He sought admission to over twenty zen monasteries, but none of them allowed him to stay. Finally when he was about forty he called on zen master Yohan at Choan; as soon as Yohan saw him he understood Shinryu's spirit and admitted him. He tested him with the story of Zhaozhou checking on the old woman.*

Shinryu saw that Yohan had the will to lead the community and deeply believed in him and submitted to him, with no desire to go anywhere else. He immersed himself in study with utmost seriousness; he didn't lie down for years. One day, hauling firewood during general labor, as he strained to lift a bundle he had a powerful insight; he hurried to the abbot's room to tell Yohan. Yohan gave him the seal of recognition and entrusted the teaching and temple affairs to him.

Before long, the patrons and community submitted to Shinryu, even more than the former teacher; they added fields and gardens and rebuilt the halls, thereby greatly

---

* There was a woman in north China who lived on the way to Mt. Wu Tai, a famous holy mountain and place of pilgrimage; whenever a monk would ask her the way to Mt. Wu Tai, she would say "Right straight ahead." As the monk set off, she would say, "A fine priest! He too goes on this way." Someone reported this to Zhaozhou, the greatest zen master in northern China in that time; he said, "Wait till I check out that old woman." He went and asked her the same thing, and she gave the same answer. Zhaozhou said, "I have checked out that old woman for you." This koan appears in the *Wumenguan (Mumonkan)* and *Congronglu (Shoyoroku)*.

renovating Choan monastery. Shinryu used to say to the community, "The important thing in buddhism is to meet the hammer and tongs of a true teacher; once I heard my late teacher's instruction, I lost my mouth and ears and have been cool ever since. Don't pass the years in the mountains taking it easy."

Late in life, after entrusting the teaching to his successors, he took leave of the community and left — no one knew where he ended up. The present shrine at Tomikawa was set up out of respect for his virtue by people of later times.

Donju of Choan

The zen master's initiatory name was Donju; he was styled Reizan. He was from Awa prefecture. As a youth he left the dusts of the world and went to Choan monastery to follow zen master Yohan, where he had his head shaved and received the precepts. He was extremely brilliant by nature and fondly occupied himself reading; he studied widely in the inner (buddhist) and outer (confucian) classics.

One day he sighed to himself, "One who abandons society and home regards the fullfillment of buddhahood as fundamental; who am I, to indulge in reading? The classics are inexhaustible." At this point he concentrated solely on meditation. He left to seek certainty everywhere. Again he lamented, "I have traveled through much of the country looking for a teacher, wasting my mental energy. What is the use of traveling around?" Then he returned.

Yohan asked him, "How many years have you been away?" He said, "Ten years." Yohan said, "Where did you go?" He said, "Through half the country." Yohan said, "What did you understand?" Reizan had no reply. Yohan said, "Give me back the price of your sandals." Reizan suddenly had insight; afterwards he functioned responsively without trouble, unhindered at all times.

When Yohan had Shinryu succeed him, Reizan served as Shinryu's secretary and kept the same job for ten years. One day Shinryu said to him, "Since I was cursed by my late teacher, I will surely grow old in this monastery; now you too are cursed by me; you should end your life here." Then he entrusted the teaching to him and left. Then the patrons and the old worthies combined efforts to keep him there.

The master was always of solitary mien and could not be presumed upon. Travelers passing through could not become familiar with him for years. At the end he gathered the community, gave them his last admonitions, wrote a verse and died sitting. The verse said,

> Sleeping at night, rushing by day,
> For fifty-six years.
> When the eyes go blind
> I attain this great meditation.

Den'etsu of Choan

The zen master's initiatory name was Den'etsu; he was styled Chogan. It is not known where he was from. As a youth he left lay life and entered Choan monastery with zen master Yohan as his teacher. He was naturally austere and ascetic; he hauled firewood, drew water, begged for rice, and made charcoal, for twenty years, working harder than anyone else. Yohan always called him 'the reincarnated ascetic (Mahakasyapa).*

Later when Yohan had Shinryu succeed him, Den'etsu served as chief cook for Shinryu, working hard as before. One day Shinryu, passing the kitchen, found him washing rice himself; he asked, "What dirt is there in the rice?" Den'etsu said, "The chaff is endless." Shinryu said, "If it is endless, how can you wash it away?" Hearing this, Den'etsu stood transfixed; at that moment secretary Donju, standing beside Shinryu, said, "Now cook Den'etsu can really wash the rice." At these words the master was suddenly enlightened; he intoned a verse saying,

> So many years I've washed dirt;
> Today I've reached where there is no dust.
> The rice filling the bushel
> I see is the original mind.

Shinryu joyfully said, "Your teacher is brother Donju; later you should assist him in the teaching, causing our school to flourish."

Later when Shinryu had secretary Donju assume the abbacy, the master Den'etsu was placed in the senior seat. After a long time he appeared in the world at Choan; when he opened the hall and offered incense, he rightly gave thanks to zen master Donju for the milk of the teaching.

---

* Mahakasyapa, one of the Buddha Gautama's ten foremost disciples, was most excellent in the practice of asceticism; he is considered the first patriarch of zen in India, having received the personal seal of recognition from the Buddha on Vulture Peak (Grdhakuta, also sometimes 'Spiritual Mountain').

Denjo of Choan

The zen master's initiatory name was Denjo; in the community he was called the Inheritor of the School as an epithet of praise. There is no record of where he was born.

He first called on zen master Den'etsu at Choan and asked, "How should a student use his mind?" Den'etsu extended his hands and said, "Bring me your mind." Denjo was totally at a loss; Den'etsu slapped him on the face and said, "What mind do you want to use?" At these words Denjo got the message; thereupon he broke his staff and stayed there for nineteen years, so earnest that he never went outside the gate. Then he wrote a verse saying,

> A thousand miles in search of a teacher
> I came to Tomikawa;
> With no way to use the mind
> At last I meditate in peace.
> I don't know how many cushions
> I have worn out,
> Staying here for nineteen years
> At a single stretch.

Den'etsu used to say to those around him that Denjo had attained the true source, so in the community he was called the Inheritor of the School.* After Den'etsu died, the patrons asked master Denjo to succeed to his seat; the master declined, saying he had little wisdom, but they insisted again and again, reminding him of the words "he has inherited my true school." The master shed tears and couldn't refuse any more. So he set up a portrait of his late teacher in the abbot's room and bowed to it in the morn-

* The word for 'school' or 'sect' basically means 'source.'

ing and saluted it at night, just as when he was alive. The master remained in the 'relative state' for the rest of his life.*

* The position of teacher and disciple is likened to 'absolute' and 'relative.' Denjo never occupied the hojo, or abbot's quarters, keeping the position of disciple out of reverence for his teacher Den'etsu.

Senteki of Kinryu

The zen master's initiatory name was Senteki; he called himself The Man of the Ancient Mountain. He was from Musashi. He left home and society as a boy. A man of outstanding capabilities, he could see right through people.

He thought to himself, "A monk is someone who is untrammelled—why stay by an old tree stump and uselessly stick to a small byway?" So he became determined to study zen and went to the famous monasteries in eastern Japan. Wherever he went he bowled them over with his talk about the teaching; people recognized him as an accomplished student.

Finally he called on zen master Denjo at Choan; with bare feet and head, he pounded rice and hoed the garden for twenty years at a stretch. One day he heard Denjo say in the teaching hall, "'Bodhidharma did not come to China; the second patriarch did not go to India;' herein there is a silver mountain, an iron wall — when spring somes the birds call and the flowers bloom." Suddenly he had insight; he went right to the abbot's room and asked for approval. Denjo asked, "Later if someone asks about the vehicle of the school of the To succession, how will you answer?" He replied, "The white reed flowers have no different color; white birds alight on a sandbar." Denjo deeply approved of this; thereupon he warned him, "Our school will flourish greatly with you, but I fear it will be hard to find a successor." The master Senteki bowed and withdrew.

When Denjo died he inherited his seat and appeared in the world at Choan; before long his fame stirred the monasteries. At that time, the prime minister Hidetada, hearing of the master's fame in the way, made offerings to him in Edo (Tokyo), the capital city; the master talked about the teaching for the minister; delighted, the minister presented him with rare silks and saw him back to the mountain. Later the chancellor Toshitsune had a big zen monastery built at Kanazawa, which he named Tentoku, 'Heavenly Virtue.' As he was looking for a sage to be abbot there, he asked prime minister Hidetada, who recommended that he invite the master Senteki to dwell there. The chancellor sent some knights to urgently invite him, but the master did not reply. At this point the prime minister himself told the master that the chancellor's request was sincere; the master could not refuse, and after all went to begin teaching there. He greatly revived the Soto school, and people came from all over the country; the names in the monastery register numbered over five thousand.

A monk asked, "What is the master's family style?" He said, "Eating meat, cursing Shakyamuni, drunk on wine, beating up Maitreya."

The master was basically simple and did not like finery and ostentation. He kept an old horse which he used instead of a carriage; people laughed at him, but he went his own way. Once he had a slight illness and realized in himself that he would never recover, so he sent his bamboo sceptre to his disciple Kosatsu at Choan with a note saying, "After I die there will be a man beyond measure who will cause my way to flourish greatly. Hand this noseless black snake to him in my stead as a token of surety." After writing this he died sitting upright.

Guon of Kinryu

The zen master's name was Guon; he was styled Ryusui. He called himself by a different name, 'The Old Man of South Mountain.' He was from Kaga prefecture. As a youth he had his head shaved at Josho temple in his native province. He was naturally open and kind; his face never showed any anger, and all who saw him felt at ease with him.

During his traveling days he called on seven or eight teachers and understood their manners and character; there was no difference in their teachings. Sure of himself, he appeared in the world at Sosen and Ryumon monasteries, giving instructions on request to the groups there for five to seven years, gaining the status of an abbot.

One night the master thought, "If one considers a little bit to be enough in the investigation of zen, perhaps there may be something one still has not learned. I hear that zen master (Ingen) Ryuki of Obaku has come from China to Japan and is staying in Nagasaki; a perfect man is not far — I should go knock at his mysterious gate." Then he set out to go there; but though he entered Ingen's room to seek and inquire, because of the difference in language there was a lack of communication and he didn't get through the difficult, confusing points. He just worked by himself on scrupulous refinement of meditation, but even after three years had passed he still had found no way of entry. He lamented, "My affinity with buddhism in this life is not yet ripe — what is the benefit of exerting mental power in the wrong way?" so he took his leave and departed.

At that time the abbacy of Tentoku monastery was vacant, and the patrons and community there invited the master, who stayed there, going along with circumstances. One morning when he went into the shrine to bow before the buddha image, to the east he saw the sunlight shining on the tree branches; as he suddenly moved his eyes his insight opened. Thereupon he spoke a verse;

> For thirty years I have expended my spirit in vain;
> Sweeping away useless dust instead became dust itself.
> Raising my head, it meets my eyes, without any obscurity —
> Myriad forms are especially new.

The master also thought, "Realization without making sure of right and wrong is of dubious benefit." Then he led his followers to call on zen master Kosatsu at Choan. As soon as Kosatsu saw him, he received him with an individual chair, and entrusted the teaching to him according to his late teacher's will. The master bowed and accepted it, then returned to his temple.

Before long both lay people as well as monks and nuns gathered there like clouds, just as Senteki had foretold. One day as the master was going to teach in Kyoto, he passed by Mt. Obaku on the way and went to see zen master Ingen Ryuki again; Ryuki greeted him joyfully and burned incense in a special censer. The next day they had a meeting of minds and Ryuki presented him with a verse:

166

Wrapped up, carefully stored,
When it is let out in response to the situation
It is totally new.

Zen master Shoto of Zozan, who was there at Ryuki's side, had a verse which said,

An iron forehead, a copper crown —
I am glad of this chance meeting;
With tracks like the wind of lightening feet,
He expresses our affinity in action.

In 1670 the master saw me, Geppa Doin, at Kanzan; I met him with proper respect and questioned him closely about this matter. Our actions and words were in mutual accord. As I was about to go, the master took my hand and said, "The time is come; don't keep your hands in your sleeves (inactive)." Then I knew for the first time I had a teacher.

End of Biographical Extracts of the Original Stream

Manzan's Notes on Practice

Manzan and his disciple Menzan were distinguished Soto zen masters whose lineage survives today; the following notes to individuals are taken from a set of such notes in the *Zenshu seiten,* or zen bible, compiled by Arima Takudo in this century.

TO ZEN MAN FUKAN ('NOT LACKING')

The great teacher who was the third patriarch of zen said, "Complete like empty space, lacking nothing, no excess." But what is he calling 'complete?' It is the 'mind of faith' in the title to the poem from which this saying is taken, the 'ultimate way' mentioned in the first line of the poem.

The ultimate way is the one real great way, the mind of faith is the non-dualistic inconceivable mind. Mind and the way do not decrease when in illusion nor increase when in enlightenment; everything is perfect reality, each particular is complete — you can't grasp or reject anything.

However, even so, "if you do not practice it, it will not become manifest; if you do not realize it, you cannot attain it." It is like having a jewel hidden in your pocket and suffering for want of food and clothing.

Practice and realization are not nonexistent; you should start right away. Just sitting is called real practice, the freedom and ease of body and mind is called true realization.

Once practice and realization are actually fulfilled, after that you must attain to the meaning of the completeness, without lack or excess, of this way, this mind.

The zen man Fukan presented paper asking for words about dharma, so I wrote this as a help to practical investigation; take heed.

TO ZEN MAN BOKUSHIN ('SIMPLE MIND')

Silver mountain, iron wall, just sitting only; simplicity is the mind, nonadornment is basic. One flavor, pure and real, aloof of all appearances, not flowing into second thoughts, nostrils right, present in the community like a mountain — this is what is called a real patchrobed monk, or one exalted beyond things.

Bokushin is also called Mumon ('no ornament') — he wanted me to write some words of instruction based on his name, so I wrote this and gave it to him. If you want to be such a man, you must cultivate such a thing. Work on this.

TO ZEN MAN ENKAI ('PERFECT OCEAN')

Great perfect awareness is the ocean of ultimate peace; still and silent, myriad forms and images reflect therein. Yet suddenly when the wind of objects arises it turns into an ocean of birth and death, with waves of consciousnesses and feelings billowing day and night, where all sentient beings appear and disappear, with no end in sight. Although the two oceans seem different, really they come from the same source, mind. Originally there is no sign of distinction in the mind source; life and death and nirvana all revert to the essential nature of the source.

Therefore, when you realize the mind-source, the whole universe is a great round perfect ocean. But how to realize the mind source? You must liberate body and mind on the sitting cushion before you can do so.

NOTE TO TRANSLATION

In translation between languages with completely different writing systems and very different sound systems, the transliteration of names has always been difficult. The names of Chinese people in this book are transcribed in Pinyin latinization, which avoids confusion between common voiced and unvoiced consonants, such as represented in English (and Pinyin) by d and t, b and p, etc. Since the sound systems of Chinese and English differ and the pronunciation of roman letters in English is not regular in a way that can be reproduced consistently at face value in representing Chinese in roman letters with English values, certain letters unavoidably have environmental modifications in value which otherwise would have to be represented in the adoption of special conventions in any case.

In this system, the letters C, Q, X, Z Zh are of special note: C resembles TS in catsup, Q resembles CH in cheer, X resembles S in sure, Z resembles DZ in adze, Zh resembles DG in judge.

Other consonants, except r, are similar to English. R is perhaps most difficult for English speakers; it is like a simultaneous combination of r in roll and s in leisure.

An i, as final letter of a syllable beginning with ch, sh, zh, or r, sounds like er in her. Two-syllable names are elided as one word; hence the name Shitou, for example, sounds like the English words shir toe.

Final i following c, s, or z, sounds like u in put.

Elsewhere i is as in Italian.

A fuller description of spelling and pronunciation is included at the back of the book.

Note that monks usually had at least two names in China and three in Japan, one or more, often the most common, referring to the place they taught, be it a monastery name or the name of a mountain (-shan, -san/-zan). In Japan, however, many names including "mountain" did not necessarily refer to concrete mountains as places of physical abode as they usually did in China. As teachers were sometimes associated with diverse places and different teachers associated with one place at different times, names can become confusing, and we have tried to simplify reference without necessarily reflecting historical sequence in the calling of names and titles.

GUIDE TO CHINESE PRONUNCIATION AND PINYIN ORTHOGRAPHY

Pinyin	Wade-Giles	English approximations (underlined letters)
a	a	ah, (in Pinyin also g<u>e</u>t after front vowels i, u, y)
b	p	<u>b</u>
c	ts' tz'	ca<u>ts</u>up
ch	ch'	<u>ch</u> (in Pinyin used before back vowels a, u, o)
d	t	<u>d</u>
e	e, o	b<u>u</u>t (in Pinyin g<u>e</u>t after front vowels)
f	f	<u>f</u>
g	k	<u>g</u>et
h	h	<u>h</u> (in W-G, silent after e, ih sounds like -<u>er</u>)
i	i (u, ih)	p<u>i</u>n to mach<u>i</u>ne (p<u>u</u>t in PY after s, c, z; h<u>er</u> after ch, sh, zh, r)
j	ch	<u>jy, jw</u> (in PY before front vowels)
k	k'	<u>k</u>
l	l	<u>l</u>
m	m	<u>m</u>
n	n	<u>n</u>
o	o	medial in PY, l<u>oo</u>k; final, th<u>aw</u>
p	p'	<u>p</u>
q	ch'	<u>ch</u> (y/w) in PY before front/umlauted vowels
r	j	<u>r</u> (tinged with French j; a retroflex)
s	s	<u>s</u>
sh	sh	<u>sh</u> before back vowels
t	t'	<u>t</u>
u	u	b<u>oo</u>t as final
w	w	<u>w</u>
x	hs	<u>sh</u>e before front/umlaut vowels
y	y	<u>y</u>
z	tz, ts	a<u>dz</u>e

DIPTHONGS AND FINALS

Pinyin	Wade-Giles	English
ai	ai	eye
an*	an	pond *(yan, ian, sound like yen)
ao	ao	ow
ei	ei	way
en	en	honey
eng	eng	tongue
er	erh	are
ia	ia	ya
ie	ieh	yet
iu	iu	you (u tends to become slightly back and rounded, tending towards home)
ian	ian	yen
iang	iang	gong
ua	ua	waffle
uan*	uan	bond *(wen after umlaut u, *i.e.* qu, xu xu, yu)
uang	uang	wong
ui*	ui; uei*	way (in both Chinese systems, if this is both initial and final, it is written wei)
uo	uo, o	warp

u is sometimes umlauted after y, l, aways after x, q,

o/e*	o/e*	but *(may tend to bought in some cases and places)
ou	u	throw
ong	ung	o/u sounds like put

PRONUNCIATION GUIDE
TO NAMES USED IN TEXT

Pinyin	*Wade-Giles*	*Japanese*
Baiyan	Pai yen	Hakugan
Baizhang Huaihai	Po chang Huai hai	Hyakujō Ekai
Baoci	Pao tz'u	Hōji
Baqiao	Ba ch'iao	Bashō
Baofu	Pao fu	Hōfuku
Caoshan Benji	Ts'ao shan Pen chi	Sōzan Honjaku
Changlu Zhenxie	Ch'ang lu Chen hsieh	Chōrō Shinketsu
	Ch'ing liao	Seiryo
Changsha	Ch'ang-sha	Chōsha
Che of Dagui	Ta kuei Ch'e	Daī Tetsu
Daci	Ta tz'u	Daiji
Damei	Ta mei	Daibai
Danxia Zichun	Tan hsia Tzu ch'un	Tanka Shijun
Daoxin	Tao hsin	Dōshin
Daowu	Tao wu	Dōgo
Dayang Mingan	Ta yang Ming an	Daiyō Myōan
Dayang Qingxuan	Ta yang Ch'ing hsüan	Daiyō Keigen
Deshan	Te shan	Tokusan
Dongshan Liangjie	Tung shan Liang chieh	Tōzan Ryokai
Ehu	E hu	Gachō
Fayan	Fa yen	Hōgen
Fengxue	Fêng-hsüeh	Fūketsu
Furong Daokai	Fu jung Tao k'ai	Fuyō Dōkai
Fushan Fayuan	Fu shan Fa yüan	Fuzan Hōen
Guishan Lingyou	Kuei shan Ling yu	Isan Reiyū
Haojian of Xinkai	Hao chien of Hsin k'ai	Haryo
Hongren	Hung jên	Kōnin
Hongzhi Zhenjue	Hung chih Chen chueh	Wanshi Shōgaku

173

Pinyin	Wade-Giles	Japanese
Huangbo	Huang po	Obaku
Huike	Hui k'o	Eka
Jianfeng	Chien feng	Kembō
Liangshan	Liang shan	Ryōzan
Lingmo	Ling mo	Reimoku
Linji	Lin chi	Rinzai
Linquan Conglun	Lin ch'üan Ts'ung lun	Rinsen Jūrin
Longshan (Yinshan)	Lung shan	Ryūzan (Inzan)
Luopu	Luo p'u	Rakuho
Luxuan	Lu hsuan	Rokkō
Mazu	Ma tsu	Baso
Mi Shibo	Mi Shih-po	Misshihaku
Nanyue (Hengyue)	Nan yüeh	Nangaku
Nanquan Puyuan	Nan ch'uan P'u yuan	Nansen Fugan
Qinglin	Ch'ing lin	Seirin
Qingyuan Xingsi	Ch'ing-yüan Hsing ssu	Seigen Gyōshi
Rujing	Ju ching	Nyojō
Sengcan	Sêng-ts'an	Sōzan
Sengzhao	Seng chao	Sōjō
Shanshan	Shanshan	Sansan
Shengmo	Sheng mo	Shōmoku
Shishuang	Shih shuang	Sekisō
Shitou Xiqian	Shih t'ou Hsi ch'ien	Sekitō Kisen
Su Tungpo	Su T'ung p'o	Sō Tōba
Sushan	Su shan	Sōzan
Tienhuang Daowu	T'ien huang Tao wu	Tennō Dōgo
Touzi Yiqing	T'ou tzu I ch'ing	Tōsu Gisei
Wansong Xingxiu	Wansung Hsinghsiu	Banshō Gyōshū
Wuxie	Wu hsieh	
Wuzu	Wu tzu	Goso

Pinyin	Wade-Giles	Japanese
Xiangyan	Hsiang yen	Kyōgen
Xuantai	Hsuan t'ai	Gentai
Xuefeng	Hsueh feng	Seppō
Xuedou Zhijian	Hsüeh-tou Chih chien	Setchō Chikan
Xueyuan	Hsüeh-yüan	Setsugen
Yangshan	Yang-shan	Gyōzan
Yantou	Yen t'ou	Gantō
Yaoshan Weiyen	Yao shan Wei yen	Yakusan Igen
Yunju Daoying	Yun chu Tao ying	Ungo Dōyō
Yunmen	Yun men	Ummon
Yunyan	Yun yen	Ungan
Zhaozhou	Chao chou	Jōshū

NAMES OF JAPANESE ZEN MASTERS APPEARING IN *BIOGRAPHICAL EXTRACTS FROM THE ORIGINAL STREAM*

Monastery	Name(s)	Monastery	Name(s)
Eihei	Dogen Kigen	Choan	Eiko (Jutenmin)
Eihei	Koun Ejo	Tocho	Ryoshu Gensaku
Daijo	Tettsu Gikai	Ankoku	Ten'o Zenban
Yoko	Keizan Jokin	Kosho	Eshu Shutan
Soji	Gasan Soseki	Ryuko	Zukuo Soden
Yotaku	Tsugen Jakurei	Choan	Goten Yohan
Saijo	Ryoan Emyo	Choan	Shinryu (Daiunshi)
Daiji	Taiko Myoso	Choan	Reizan Donju
Saijo	Goho Sosan	Choan	Chogan Den'etsu
Kogon	Unshu Soryu	Choan	Denjo (Tekishu)
Tennei	Ikke Bun'ei	Kinryu	Senteki (Kosanjin)
Bansho	Muteki Koken	Kinryu	Ryusui Guon

GUIDE TO JAPANESE PRONUNCIATION

Japanese pronunciation and orthography in Roman is comparatively simply related to English usage; only the differences or necessary specifications in English use of letters and their use in rendering Japanese names. Length affects quantity; it is longer, with the same tone. Japanese is usually known for the purity and simplicity of its vowels, but there are some cases of subtle gradations.

Japanese	English
a	c<u>a</u>r
e	b<u>e</u>t
i	p<u>i</u>n to mach<u>i</u>ne
o	n<u>o</u>
r	no english equivalent; tongue is briefly close to the ridge between the upper palate and teeth
u	p<u>u</u>t to f<u>oo</u>l
ai	<u>eye</u>
ao	<u>ow</u> (voicing begins from the back of the mouth)
iu	<u>you</u>
ei	<u>way</u>

Front vowels, i and u, are unvoiced ('whispered') between unvoiced consonants, sh, k, ts; e.g., tsuka is pronounced ts'ka. This tendency is sometimes mitigated in difficult situations (like a run of three or so whispered vowels and unvoiced consonants in a row), especially in the older Kansai, or western Japanese dialects.